Mrs. Hannah Cowley

A day in Turkey

The Russian slaves

Mrs. Hannah Cowley

A day in Turkey
The Russian slaves

ISBN/EAN: 9783743316331

Manufactured in Europe, USA, Canada, Australia, Japa

Cover: Foto ©ninafisch / pixelio.de

Manufactured and distributed by brebook publishing software
(www.brebook.com)

Mrs. Hannah Cowley

A day in Turkey

A DAY IN TURKEY;

O R,

THE RUSSIAN SLAVES.

A

C O M E D

_____ LEY.

(BLIN:

MESSRS. WOGAN, BYRNE, GRUEBER,
, H. COLBERT, J. MOORE, J. JONES,
ES, M'ALLISTER, CORBET, AND
RICE.

M.DCC.XCII.

A DAY IN TURKEY;

OR,

THE RUSSIAN SLAVES,

A

COMEDY,

AS ACTED AT THE

THEATRE ROYAL,

IN

COVENT GARDEN.

———————

BY MRS. COWLEY.

———————

DUBLIN:

PRINTED FOR MESSRS. WOGAN, BYRNE, GRUEBER,
M'KENZIE, H. COLBERT, J. MOORE, J. JONES,
W. JONES, M'ALLISTER, CORBET, AND
RICE.

M.DCC.XCII.

ADVERTISEMENT.

HINTS have been thrown out, and the idea induftrioufly circulated, that the following comedy is tainted with POLITICS. I proteft I know nothing about politics;— will Mifs Wolftonecraft forgive me---whofe book contains fuch a body of mind as I hardly ever met with---if I fay that politics are *unfeminine?* I never in my life could attend to their difcuffion.

TRUE COMEDY has always been defined to be a picture of life—a record of paffing manners---a mirror to refle&t to fucceeding times the charaéters and follies of the prefent. How then could I, pretending to be a comic poet, bring an emigrant

A 3 Frenchman

ADVERTISEMENT.

Frenchman before the public at this day, and not make him hint at the events which had juſt paſſed, or were then paſſing in his native country? A character ſo written would have been anomalous---the critics ought to have had no mercy on me. It is A LA GREQUE who ſpeaks, not *I;* nor can I be accountable for *his* ſentiments. *Such* is my idea of tracing CHARACTER; and were I to continue to write for the ſtage, I ſhould always govern myſelf by it.

THE illiberal and *falſe* ſuggeſtions concerning the politics of the comedy I could frankly forgive, had they not deprived it of the honour of a COMMAND. The paſſages on which thoſe miſrepreſentations were built, were on the ſecond night omitted, but immediately afterwards reſtored; and the DAY IN TURKEY leaves the preſs exactly as it has continued to be performed amidſt the moſt vivid and uninterrupted plaudits-----or interrupted only by the glitter of ſoft tears; a ſpecies of applauſe not leſs flattering than the

ſpontaneous

ADVERTISEMENT.

ſpontaneous laugh, or the voluntary colli-
ſion of hands.

SOME of the performers in this comedy
have played ſo tranſcendently well, that
their names deſerve to be recorded; but
to particularife any, when *all* have aimed
at perfection, would be invidious.

H. COWLEY.

Feb. 17.
1792.

NOT from the prefent moment fprings our play,
Th' events which gave it birth are paft away—
Five glowing moons have chas'd night's fhades from
    earth,
Since the war fled which gave our Drama birth.
" *Not fmiling peace o'er* RUSSIA's *wide-fpread land*
" *Wav'd gently* then, *her fceptre of command.*
" *No! thoufands rufh'd at red ambition's call,*
" *With mad'ning rage to triumph—or to fall.*
" *'Twas then our female bard from* BRITAIN's *fhore*
" *Was led by fancy to the diftant roar"*——
'Twas then fhe faw fweet virgins captives made,
'Twas then fhe faw the cheek of beauty fade,
Whilft the proud foldier in ignoble chains,
Was from his country dragg'd to hoftile plains.

    Thus was her bold imagination fired
When battle with its horrid train retired;
Yet, fure the ftory which fhe then combin'd,
Should not to dear oblivion be refign'd—
No—let it ftill your various paffions raife,
And to have touch'd them, oft', has been her praife:
Trufting to candour, fhe folicits here,
Your fmile of pleafure, or your pity's tear;
For tho' the *time* is paft, the FEELING true,
She dedicates to NATURE, and to YOU!

    Note.——The lines diftinguifhed by italics are from the pen
of DELLA CRUSCA.

PERSONS of the DRAMA.

MEN.

IBRAHIM,	Mr. *HOLMAN.*
ORLOFF,	Mr. *FARREN.*
A LA GREQUE,	Mr. *FAWCET.*
MUSTAPHA,	Mr. *MUNDEN.*
AZIM,	Mr. *CUBIT.*
SELIM,	Mr. *INCLEDON.*
MULEY,	Mr. *M'CREADY.*
ISMAEL,	Mr. *FARLEY.*
OLD MAN,	Mr. *THOMPSON.*
SON,	Mr. *CROSS.*
2d TURK,	Mr. *EVATT.*

MALE SLAVES, &c.

WOMEN.

ALEXINA,	Mrs. *POPE.*
PAULINA,	Mrs. *ESTEN.*
LAURETTA.	Mrs. *MATTOCKS.*
FATIMA,	Mrs. *MARTYR.*
FEMALE SLAVES,	{ Mrs. *FAWCET,* Mrs. *ROCK,* and others.

A

DAY IN TURKEY.

ACT I.

SCENE I. *A Forest.*

IN THE BACK GROUND A TURKISH CAMP.

Several Turks are seen at a Distance passing and repassing with Haste; some of them look out from amidst the Trees, and then retire.

Enter PAULINA, *precipitately.*

At the Bottom.

PAU.

WHERE—O, where shall we fly? [*Looking round wildly.*] Brother—father—come! We are driven from our cottage: we have no longer a home —let us run some where to seek another.

Enter OLD MAN *and* SON.

SON. Come father lean on me, and let us walk faster, or we shall be pick'd up by some of the turban'd gentry. They are out a foraging; and they always consider christians as useful cattle. Let us fly.

B   FATHER.

FATHER. Fly! alas, with the load of seventy years upon my shoulders, how hard a task! We shall never escape them, child—Thou'lt see thy father murdered, and worse luck than that will be thy fate.

PAU. Worse luck than to be murdered! I should be glad to see the day—What worse *can* happen?

OLD MAN. Thou'lt be made a slave,—slave to a Turk [*cries*]—I shall see thee in a vile Turk's seraglio, no better, as it were, than the handmaid of a Jew.

PAU. Well, I may out-live such a misfortune as that; but I never heard of out-living a throat cut—So, dear father, cheer up, and let us hurry on to the next village. Peter, take care of that bag—for it contains all we have in the world.

SON. Aye; and if it hadn't been for some of our own soldiers, I had been a lost man—They were so kind as to strip our cottage yesterday, and left us no more than I can very *conveniently* move under.

PAU. Yes; and more than all that, they took away my very best gown, and my new fur cap! [*crying*] yes; and he who took them said it was in friendship, for that otherwise my very best gown and cap would certainly fall into the hands of the enemy.

SON. Yes; it was truly a very friendly action, and they perform'd it like gentlemen—No words, but their very looks were oaths, and the black eyebrows of one of them spoke louder curses than I ever heard between fifty Siberian boar-hunters [*clashing of swords without.*] There—there! d'ye hear? Our friends are coming down upon us; and our enemies are at hand! Come, let us run [*with a look of terror*]—From friends and enemies, holy Michael, defend us!

[*Exeunt.*

[*Clashing of swords;* A LA GREQUE *enters running at top, then stops, looks back and speaks.*]

A LA GR. There it goes—There it goes! Nothing can save thee, my gallant master—This comes of your reconnoitering—Had you not better have been in your tent, quietly breaking your *fast*, than here, breaking

the

the heads of the Turks—So, now he's difarm'd—
Well, nobody bid ye—'tis all your own fault—Now,
how comely he looks with his arms folded, and his
fword in the hands of that beetle-brow'd Turk!
Pardie! I feel now as great a man as my mafter.

Enter ORLOFF, *furrounded by Turks.*

MULEY. Courageous Ruffian, thou art ours!
Could valour have faved thee, captivity and you had
never met—Your emprefs, we trult, has not many fuch
foldiers in the neighbouring camp.——Come, droop
not, Sir, this is the fortune of war.

ORLOFF. Had I been made your prifoner, whilft on
a poft of duty, I could have borne my lot—A foldier
can fupport not only death, but even flaveiy, when a
fenfe of duty gives *dignity* to his chains; but *my* chains
are bafe ones, for I reconnoiter'd without command,
and have loft my liberty without glory.

A LA GR. Then *I* have loft my liberty too without glory, for I *attended* you without command, and
now—Oh, *le diable!* I am valet de chambre to a
flave!

TURK. Let not that affect thee! The fortune of
war, which has wounded your mafter's pride, ought to
elate yours, for you are now his equal—both flaves
alike.

A LA GR. [*Eagerly*] Are we fo? And has he
no further right to command me, nor threaten me?
Kind Sir, tell me but that—tell me but that—!

TURK. None, none.

A LA GR. Hum! [*Puts his hat on, takes out his
fnuff box, takes fnuff, then goes to his mafter, and
offers him his box.*] Take a pinch, don't be fly

ORLOFF. Scoundrel! [*Throws up the box with
his arm.*]

A LA GR. Nay, no hard names—let us be civil
to each other, as brother flaves ought to be—And now
I think of it—Hark ye! I fuppofe your flaves take
rank according to their ufefulnefs.

TURK. Certainly.

A LA

A LA GR. Well then, my mafter—I mean that man there, who was my mafter, can do no earthly thing but fight, whilft I, on the contrary, am expert at feveral.

MULEY. Your qualifications?

A LA GR. They are innumerable—I can fing you pretty little French airs, and Italian canzonettas—No man in Paris, Sir—for I have the honour to be a Frenchman—No man in Paris underftands the fcience of the powder-puff better than myfelf—I can frize you in a tafte beyond—Oh, what you are all CROPS, I fee—fore fronts, and back fronts—Oh, thofe vile turbans, my genius will be loft amongft you, and a frizeur will be of no more ufe than an oyfter-woman.— Why, you look as though you had all been fcalp'd, and cover'd your crowns with your pillows.

TURK. Chriftian, our turbans are too elevated a fubject for your fport.

A LA GR. Dear Sir, [pointing to his turban, and then to the ground] drop the fubject, it will be a proof of national tafte.

MULEY. Thy fpeech is licentious and empty; but in a Frenchman we can pardon it—'tis national Tafte —However, if your boafted qualifications end here, it is probable, you will be a flave as little diftinguifh'd as your mafter.

A LA GR. Pardonnez moi! I can do things he never thought of—You have heard the ftory of the bafket-maker amongft favages? I do not defpair of feeing my mafter my fervant yet—Courage, Monfieur le Compte! I'll treat you with great condefcenfion, depend on't, and endeavour to make you forget in all things the diftance between us.

MULEY. He feems too deeply abforb'd in melancholy, to be roufed by thy impertinence!

A LA GR. Poor young man! Times are alter'd, to be fure; and at prefent he's a little down in the mouth; but he's fond of mufic, cheer him with a Turkifh air—Helas! all the *air* we have will be Turkifh now.

[ORLOFF.

ORLOFF. Ah no! forbear your mufic, and bring me your chains! Drag me to your dungeons! The intellectual bitternefs of this moment cannot be increafed by *outward* circumftance.

A LA GR. Chains and dungeons! Why fure the ghoft of our dead baftille has not found its way hither —Hey, Meffieurs! Have you lantern pofts too, and hanging Marquiffes in this country?

ORLOFF. [*angrily.*] Peace!

A LA GR. Peace! That's a bold demand.—Your Emprefs can't find it at the head of a hundred thoufand men, and the moft fublime Grand Signior is obliged to put on his night-cap without it, though he has a million of thefe pretty Gentlemen to affift him—Befides, England has engrofs'd the commodity.

ORLOFF. Come, Sir, let us not loiter here—I would have my fate determined, and my mifery compleat. Alas! is it not already fo? Yes, my heart has been long the property of forrow, and it will never relinquish its claims.

MULEY. I fhall lead you to the palace of the Baffa Ibrahim—it is in the neighbourhood of yonder camp, which he commands, what your fate may then be, his humour determines.

A LA GR. Then I hope we fhall catch him in a *good* humour, and what care I whether a Turk or a Ruffian has the honour to be my mafter? Now you fee the misfortune of being born a Count! Had he loft no more than I have, he'd be as carelefs as I am —Come, brother. flave—no ceremony, no ceremony, I beg.

[*Exeunt*—A LA GREQUE *pulls back his mafter, and walks out before him.*

SCENE

SCENE II.   ROCKS.

[Enter PETER—runs acrofs the Stage, is follow'd by
PAULINA fhrieking—they go off—Two Turks pur-
fue them, and bring them back.]

TURK.   Stay, ftay, young ones! it is but manners
to wait for your father—You fee he is hobbling up as
faft as he can.

PAU.   Aye, very true—Oh, Peter, how could we
run away, and leave our father?

PETER.   Why, we only took care of number one,
and we have a right to do that all the world over.
So we are captives now then, and flaves in downright
earneft?

TURK.   Aye.

PAU.   Look at my poor father! If your hearts
were not harder than thofe very rocks, you could
never make a flave of *him.*

Enter the FATHER, *guarded by two* TURKS.

FATHER.   O my dear children! Thofe flints which
wound my feet are not fo fharp as the wounds which
gafh my heart for you.

PAU.   There!—Do ye hear? O the miferies of
war! I wonder war is ever the fafhion—Pray, Sir,
what made the King of the Turks and our old Emprefs agree to go to war together?

TURK.   To give brave foldiers an opportunity of
running away with fuch pretty girls as you.

PAU.   O fye on them! I think if they were now
to fee my father and brother Peter, and I, in this condition, they'd be both afham'd of themfelves.

PETER.   Afham'd of themfelves! Don't talk fo
ign'r'ntly.—Excufe her, gentlemen, fhe knows nothing
of the world.   She thinks Kings and Emprefles are
made of the fame ftuff as other mortals.

TURK.   [*To the Father.*]   Come, Honefty, cheer
up! at the next village there is a waggon, into which
you

you and your family fhall be put, and carried to the
end of your fhort journey.

Pau. Laws! A waggon—whofe is it?

'Turk. It fhall be your own for the prefent.

Pau. Our own! that's droll enough; fo we are
made flaves in order to ride in our own carriage.

[*Exeunt.*

SCENE. *The Gardens of the Baffa, decorated
with Palms, Fountains, &c. in the Eaftern ftyle.*

Enter Mustapha.

Mus. Where is fhe? Where is fhe? I don't fee
her here—She's generally leaning on that fountain,
looking like the nymph of the ftream, fwelling it with
her tears.

Azim. [*without.*] But I fay no—do you mark
me, I fay no—

Entering with two Slaves.

Mus. Then I fay yes, do ye mark me? What a
bawling you make—What are you coming here for,
hey?

Azim. To look for that infolent female flave,
that Ruffian, that I may manage her a little.

Mus. You manage her! Your ill humour towards
her is never to be fatisfied—You are as malicious as
you are high—Don't I know how to manage an obftinate female as well as you?

Azim. Ha, ha, ha! All the knowledge that nature
cou'd contrive to pack into that little carcafe of thine
wou'd be infufficient for fuch a purpofe—Manage an
obftinate female! The greateft generals in the world,
and the greateft tyrants have been foil'd at it—Leave
her to me—I have difcretion—fhe fhall be kept on
bread and water.

Mus. Mark his difcretion! Keep a pretty woman
on bread and water to make her contented and kind.

Azim. 'Tis right, I'll maintain it to her teeth—
for, firft, fhe is a Ruffian and a bear—

Mus.

Mus. The beautiful Alexina, a Ruffian bear! Well, secondly?

Azim.   She is a chriftian, and thofe chriftians are the moft unnaturalift creatures in the world—Why, man, they betray their friends, and love their enemies, ha, ha!

Mus.   Do they fo? Then fhe's no chriftian—for as to loving her enemies, I have heard her fay to thy face, that fhe hates thee—So, let her be treated like an honeft Turk.

Azim.   So fhe fhall—an honeft Turk returns hate for hate, and fo, d'ye fee, her feaft fhall be a faft.

[*Goes off at the top.*

Mus.   Take care of the orders I gave ye—When our mafter arrives, let no one be over bufy to fpeak of this Ruffian flave—if poffible, I would have him forget that fhe is in the Haram.

Slaves.   We fhall be careful.   [*Exeunt Slaves.*

Enter Alexina *from the top, follow'd by* Azim.

Alex.   Purfue me not, thou inexorable flave! You invade my retirement, you drive me from folitude, though folitude alone can mitigate my forrows.

Azim.   Nonfenfe—Solitude and retirement! *they* were made for birds of night; owls may rejoice in them, but women fhould feek day-light.

Alex.   Day-light gives me no joy. Through eleven weeks have I dragg'd on a torpid exiftence—See! *(going to a tree)* here is the fad regifter of my days of infelicity.   My bodkin on its tender rind hath mark'd the return of each *unhallow'd* Sabbath;—the wounds now but juft difcernible will deepen as the tree advances to maturity, and fpeak in another age, the miferies of Alexina.

[*Takes up a folded paper from amongft the fhrubs.*

A p per!—poetry! ah, how difcriptive of my own fenfations—which of my companions hath thus melodioufly fung her forrows? [*reads*]

I 2.

I a poor captive feel each day
   That flowly creeps with leaden pace,
Bleft freedom here ne'er lends her ray—
   Her bright fteps here, we never trace.

Oh that wild on fome high mountain
   I could catch the wand'ring winds,
Or ftarting from fome defert fountain,
   Emulate the bounding hinds!

The clouds that fwim in air's foft ocean,
   Seem to fcorn my prifon towers,
Zephyr's light unfetter'd motion,
   Deeper, heavier, makes my hours.

AZIM. [*fnatching the paper from her hand.*] Such a wailing about freedom and liberty! why the chriftians in one of the northern iflands have eftablifhed a flave trade, and proved by act of parliament that freedom is no blefling at all.

MUS. No, no, they have only proved that it does not fuit dark complexions. To fuch a pretty creature as this, they'd think it a blefling to *give* every freedom—and *take* every freedom.

AZIM. Come, come, be gay and happy, like the reft of the flaves. How ftands your mind to-day towards a handfome Baffa? Our mafter is returning from the camp—The ceffation of hoftilities will give him a fhort leifure, which he will certainly devote to pleafure and his haram.

ALEX. Muftapha, do not let that unfeeling flave talk to me—thou haft humanity.

MUS. Would I could adminifter to his difeafe, it is a terrible one! the love of talking is in him an abfolute frenzy! To filence him is impoffible—but as I have power over him, I can oblige him to retire—Go!

AZIM. Go! What, fhall an infolent chriftian?—

MUS. Go, go!

AZIM. She fhall repent. [*Exit.*

ALEX.

ALEX. Doth your mafter indeed return to-day?

Mus. Yes; and all the women of his harain are preparing for his reception—they, half frantic with joy, wonder to behold your tears.

ALEX. *I* am not a woman of his haram [*with difdain*]

Mus. But, charming Alexina, can you hope longer to efcape? To-day he will fee you.

[ALEXINA *ftands a moment as tho' ftruck, then clafps her bands with an action of defpair ; then turns.*]

ALEX. Oh Muftapha! behold a lowly fuppliant. [*Kneels*] She is of no vulgar rank who thus kneels to you for protection.

Mus. For protection! I am myfelf a flave—Rife, dear lady.

ALEX. [*Rifing*] But thou haft power with thy mafter. Oh! invent fome excufe—fay fomething to fave me from the interview.

Mus. I will confider—I—[*mufic at a diftance*] Nay, if it muft be fo, conceal yourfelf at once, for I hear the mufic which announces his approach; and he will probably haften hither.

ALEX. O miferable fpeed! I go—Muftapha, on thy eloquence depends my breath—The moments of my life are number'd by thy fuccefs—Prefs fearlefsly the caufe of virtue, and glow with the fainted fubject.

Thus, tho' a flave, thy foul's high ftate
   Shall prove its origin divine,
Soar far above thy wretched fate,
   And o'er thy chains fublimely fhine. [*Exit.*

Mus. Why, as to chaftity, and all that, which you make an orthodox article of, fweet one! we Turks are a fort of diffenters—a woman's virtue with us, is to CHARM, and her religion fhould be LOVE.— Ah, ha! here comes Ibrahim, and his whole haram ——*His* creed is love, and there is not a more orthodox man in the country.

Enter

Enter LAURETTA *and* FATIMA [*haſtily.*]

LAUR. Ah! Muſtapha, the Baſſa is arrived full
of triumph, full of wiſhes, panting to behold Alexina
—What will become of her? Where is ſhe?

MUS. She juſt now run off on that ſide, and I
ſhall run off on this—for I have not ſettled what to
ſay about her, and BASSAS and TYGERS are animals
not made to be trifled with.   [*Exit.*

FAT. Well, let that pretty melancholy ſlave feel
as ſhe pleaſes—I, for my part, am half out of my
wits, to think how happy we ſhall be now the Baſſa
is come back—we ſhall have nothing but whim and
entertainment.—Have you been looking at the new
pavilion to day?

LAUR. No.

FAT. O dear! it is almoſt finiſhed —The hang-
ings are gold tiſſue, and when our beautiful ſofa,
which we have been making for him is ſet up, and the
Baſſa ſees it all together, he will be tranſported.—
Do you not think ſo? Hark! here he comes with all
the enſigns of war at his heels.—O no—*they* come
firſt, I proteſt—I'll ſtand here, and take a view of the
whole.

[*A march is play'd. Standard bearers advance firſt;
they are followed by female ſlaves, who dance down
the ſtage to light muſic, and exit. The chorus ſingers
follow; female ſlaves ſtrewing flowers from little
baſkets ſucceed; the Baſſa then appears at the top
with his principal officers.*]

Chorus. SELIM, LAUR. FAT. &c.

Hark! ſound the trumpet, breathe the flute,
And touch the ſoft melodious lute :
To heav'n let ev'ry grateful ſound aſcend,
  Thanks for our prince reſtor'd,
  Our lover, and our friend.
Victorious hero! blooming ſage!
The ſcourge and glory of our age!

        Let

Let roseate pleasures round thy footsteps twine,
And lead thee on to joy,
And bless thy valiant line !
Vain breathes the trumpet and the flute,
And lost the soft melodious lute,
When, Ibrahim! thy praise they wou'd display.
Sunk in the lofty theme,
As twilight yields to day!

IBRA.   Enough of praise, and of triumph! A
sweeter triumph than your songs can bestow, awaits
me—Where is the lovely Russian, who, tho' my captive more than two moons, I have not yet beheld?

AZIM.   We rejoice in our lord's return, that her
pride may be humbled.—The insolence of her carriage, and the perverseness of her temper, are in-
tolerable.

IBRA.   Thou hast seen her, Muley, does she justify
Azim's description?

MULEY.   She is reserved, my lord, reserved and
melancholy—but she is too gentle to be insolent.

AZIM.   Muley knows her not—Canst thou believe
it, mighty Bassa, the idea of surrend'ring her charms
to thee, and of being raised to the honour of thy
notice, has never once soften'd her ill humour, nor
abated her melancholy.

IBRA.   Indeed! [*Angrily*] Bring her to me instantly—yes, instantly bid her come to my presence,
and tell her—No—hold—I will receive her in my hall
of audience, dazzle her with my greatness, and astonish
her into love.

LAUR.   Ha, ha, ha! Ha, ha, ha!

IBRA.   Why that laugh, Lauretta?

LAUR.   Ha, ha, ha! at your new invention of
astonishing people into love.—If you can contrive to
do that, you will be the most astonishing *Bashaw* in
all Turkey.

IBRA.   How then?

LAUR.   Grandeur and dignity to inspire love! Ha,
ha, ha! they may inspire your pretty captive with
veneration and respect—but veneration and respect is
an atmosphere so cold, that loves starves in it.

IBRA.

IBRA. What then muft I do to touch her heart with love?

LAUR. Affect humility; not greatnefs. You muft become a fuppliant, before you can hope to be a victor.

IBRA. Doft thou fpeak truth, my pretty Italian? —Thy country is the country of love, and thou fhould'ft be an adept in the fcience.

LAUR. Yes; I know the hiftory of the heart, and do affure you, that you muft become the flave of your captive, if you ever mean to tafte the fublime exceffes of a mutual paffion.

AZIM. [contemptuoufly] Mutual paffion! Sir, fhe is your flave, command her! Such bafenefs may befit an Italian, but a muffulman is more fenfible to his dignity.

IBRA. I will hear you both further on the fubject —The iron labour of the war is for a few weeks fuf-pended—and during that ceffation, Pleafure! I am thine. Prepare your banquets, compofe new delights, let every hour teem with frefh-invented joys, till I forget the toils of the fanguinary field, and bathe my wounds with rofy-finger'd love.

[Exit with part of his train.

FAT. Well, he's in delightful fpirits—But how ftrange it is that the Ruffian flave fhou'd not have prefented herfelf to welcome her mafter, and to give him an impreffion of her charms.

LAUR. Stranger if fhe had, when nothing frightens her fo much as the idea of infpiring him with a paffion —I am interefted for her, and it is for this reafon I fhall endeavour to make Ibrahim purfue a conduct not ufual from a mighty muffulman to his flave.

[Exit.

FAT. Hark ye, Azim! What makes your lovely countenance look fo grim, when we are all fo gay? I declare your glum face fuits the day as little as a black patch upon a gold robe—Change it, man, change it! and don't be afraid of lofing any thing by it, for you muft look carefully to pick up a worfe.

[Exit.

C

MULEY.

MULEY.   Azim, since I saw thee last, I have trod the paths of glory—I have slumbered amidst the frosts of the night, I have toil'd amidst the streams of burning day; but I return and find thee the same.—With me all things have chang'd, but thou art unalter'd.— Thy temper, like the deep shadow of the forest, is sometimes chequer'd by the dart of the angry lightning, but the serene cheerfulness of the morning dwells not with thee.

AZIM.   Well, and what then? If you like me not, thwart me not.   There's room enough in Turkey for thee and for me.—Let the crow and the vulture rest on the same tree; but may thou and I live as far apart as the streams of Ilyssus, and the waters of the Bosphorus.

SELIM.   Surely thy evil disposition must be a scourge to thy soul—it must be affliction to thee.

SONG, SELIM.

Ah! teach thy breast soft pity's throb,
  And harmonize thy rugged mind,
Ah! teach thy lid soft pity's tear,
  That gem of sentiment refined.
Could'st thou once know the tender bliss
  The sympathizing bosom knows,
When at meek sorrow's sacred touch,
  Responsive sadness round it flows—
No more thy brow wou'd wear that frown,
  Thy glance no more so sternly dart,
But joys would glitter in thy eye,
  And peace cling gladly to thy heart.
                                 [*Exeunt.*

END OF THE FIRST ACT.

ACT II.

SCENE *An Apartment in the* BASSA'*s Palace.*

IBRAHIM *discovered, seated under a Canopy, Officers
and Slaves attending.*

Enter MULEY.

IBRA. SAY, valiant Muley, where are your pri-
foners ?

MULEY. Waiting at your threfhold for admittance.

IBRA. Are they of rank ?

MULEY. I fufpect one of them conceals his rank
with the hopes of lowering his ranfom—the other is
his fervant.

IBRA. Bring them before me.   [*Exit* MULEY.

Re enter MULEY *with* ORLOFF *and* A LA GREQUE.

IBRA. Who *are* you ?

ORLOFF. A foldier.

IBRA. The enemy of our faith.

ORLOFF. The enemy of thofe only who oppofe
the interefts of my fovereign—To chaftize them I
this morning bore a fword which your flaves won
from me, hardly ! Let them confider it as the nobleft
acquifition of the day.

IBRA. Chriftian, this air of intrepidity, when
amidft the foldiers of the Ruffian camp, might have
fuited thy condition ; thou art now a flave thyfelf,
acquire then that humility which becomes thy ftate.

ORLOFF. Difhonourable ! I demand my liberty.
—A truce has been proclaim'd, and——

IBRA. Not till after thou wert captured ; thou
art, therefore, by the laws of arms, fairly our pri-

C 2   foner.

foner.—Give him the flave's habit, and fet him to labour. Who art *thou?*

A la Gr. Not a Ruffian, dear Sir, 'pon my honour, nor the enemy of your faith; I believe it's a very genteel faith, and I have all the refpect in the world for Turkifh gentlemen.—I never faw prettier behav'd, prettier diefs'd people in my life—they have as much politenefs and good breeding as tho' they were my own countrymen.

Ibra. Of what country are thou?

A la Gr. Oh, Paris, Sir, Paris. I travell'd into Ruffia to polifh the brutes a little, and to give them fome ideas of the general equality of man ; but my generofity has been loft ;—they ftill continue to believe that a prince is more than a porter, and that a lord is a better gentleman than his flave. O, had they but been with me at Verfailles, when I help'd to turn thofe things topfey turvey there!

Ibra. Did you find them equally dull in other refpects.

A la Gr. ˉ Yes. Finding they would not learn liberty, I would have taught them dancing, but they feem'd as incapable of one bleffing as the other ; fo, now *I* am led a dance by this gentleman [*turning to his mafter*] into your chains, in which, if I can but dance myfelf into your favour, I fhall think it the beft *ftep* I ever took.

Ibra. The freedom of thy fpeech does not difpleafe me.

A la Gr. Dear Sir, I am your moft obedient humble flave, ready to bow my head to your fandals, and to lick the duft from your beautiful feet.

Ibra. Ha, ha, ha!

A la Gr. Ah, ah!—ça ira!—ça ira! [*fpringing*]

Ibra. Go, take thy late mafter into thy protection, and fee if thou canft infpire him with thy own good humour ; his chains will be the lighter.

A la Gr. Oh Sir, as to chains, I value them not a rufh; if it is your highnefs's fweet pleafure to load me with them, I fhall be thankful for the honour, and dance to their clink—Blefs ye, Sir,

chains

chains were as natural t'other day to *Frenchmen* as mother's milk.

IBRA. Take them away.

[*Exit* ORLOFF, A LA GREQUE, *&c.*

IBRA. Well, Azim, where is this lovely Ruffian?

Enter AZIM.

AZIM. Mighty lord, thy fervant dares fcarce pronounce his errand.—She refufes to come.

IBRA. How!

AZIM. I delivered your commands, I ordered her on pain of death to appear inftantly befoie you, yet fhe ftill refufes. She talks of her facred honour, and I know not what.

IBRA. [*Paufing*] Cold,—unimpaffion'd,—not to be awed,—and a facred regard for her honour—Then, at length, I fhall tafte the joy of overcoming RESISTANCE. [*with an action of pleafure*]

AZIM. What means my lord?

IBRA. I am fatiated, I am tired with the dull acquiefcence of our eaftein flaves, and rejoice that I have at length found one, who will teach me to hope and to *defpair*

AZIM. Mighty Baffa, fhe will have the infolence to defpife equally your threats and your love—Punifhment ought to be infl cted.

IBRA. Beware how thou endeavoureft to weaken her hauteur! I will abate nothing of her inflexibility, I will be enamour'd of fcorn, her cruelty fhall be my triumph.

Enter LAURETTA.

AZIM. I fay then, my Lord.

IBRA. What! am I to be oppofed—retire, flave!

LAUR. Why do you not go? have you nor leave to depart? Come, try the frefh air, Goodman Whifkers. (*pulling him out by the fleeve*) I declare, my Lord, that bufy medling flave is not able to c nduct an affair of this fort—but, Sir, if you will follow my advice, I'll engage—

C 3   IBRA.

IBRA. I'll follow *no* advice—My heart fpurns at *inftruÆions*, and equally contemns both your leffons and his—

LAUR. Upon my word, he's advanc'd a great way in a fhort time—follow no advice! [*afide*]

IBRA. There is a tranfport which I have never yet experienc'd, but which my foul longs to poffefs—Yes, my heart languifhes to remove the timid veil of coynefs, to foften by fweet degrees, the ice of chaftity, and to fee for once, referve facrificed at the altar of tendernefs ; *thefe,* cruel Love ! are luxuries thou haft never yet beftowed on me. [*Exit.*

LAUR. So, fo! 'tis dangerous to give fome people a hint, I find—I thought to have held the mafter-fpring, and to have managed him like a puppet ; but prefto! he's out of fight before I knew I had loft him, and leaves his inftructor groveling behind—I muft feek fome other field for my talents. I fee. [*confidering*] Yes, I think, I think that may do—Muley, and the other four, with our little Muftapha—Yes, yes ; with thefe half dozen, I'll weave a webb of amufement to crack the fides of a dozen gloomy harems with laughter—Mercy! what a fleepy life wou'd our valiant Baffa and his damfels lead, but for my talents at invention. [*Exit.*

SCENE   *The Garden.*

Enter MUSTAPHA, AZIM, *and* FATIMA.

MUS. All thy malice is not worth that. [*fnapping his fingers.*]

FAT. That's right, my little Muftapha, [*patting him on the fhoulder*] don't mind him ; he's never happy, but when he's plaguing fomebody—What has the pretty Ruffian done to you, that you fhould be fo fet on making her wretched?

MUS. I tell thee Alexina fhall not be made miferable whilft I have a hair in my beard.

FAT. There, do you hear, Mr. Sour Chops ? I am fure if all the flaves who have the care of us, had your ill-nature, I had rather fink down into the condition

dition of a water-carrier, than live in a great man's harem.

Azim. I tell thee, that should she become the favourite flave, thou will repent thy blind prejudice—We shall then all be in her power—tremble at her revenge.

Mus. Tremble thou, whofe perfecutions will make thee a proper object of her revenge—for me, what will she have to return me but offices of refpect and kindnefs? Go, go, thy turbulent fpirit makes thee hateful.

Voice [without] Fatima! Fatima!

Fat. I'll come inftantly—And you shall come with me. [running up to Azim] Nay, 'tis in vain to refift, there is a dozen of us in the next walk, and we'll mould you into a better temper'd monfter before we have done with you, I warrant. Selima! Bafca! come and help me.

Mus. Begone, I fay.

Fat. O, what you move, do you? The creature is mended already. [Exit, dragging out Azim.

Mus. So, my Lord Baffa, that hafty ftep, and that eager look proclaim thy errand—I know thou wilt catch the bird at laft; but I will keep the little flutterer from thee as long as I can.

Enter IBRAHIM, [haftily].

Ibra. Where is the Ruffian flave? the women tell me she fpends her hours in my garden, but I cannot fee her here, though her fragrant breath feems to falute me from the rofe trees, and her melodious voice from amidft the bushes, where the painted fongfters pour forth their ftrains. Where is she, Muftapha?

Mus. I faw her awhile ago at the right there fomewhere, but may be she's at the left by this time——There's no gueffing.

Ibra. Azim complains that she is an infolent and fcornful beauty, not gentle, nor complaifant in the leaft.

Mus.

Mus. I'll follow the lead, and destroy every wish he may have to behold her [aside] Yes, yes; as to insolence, match me her fellow if you can—Bless us, to see the difference! Why, my Lord, our Eastern beauties are so gentle, so complying, they scarcely give you time to wish.

Ibra. Thou say'st right [smiling].

Mus. Pretty creatures! if a man does but look at them, they drop like a ripe cherry from the bough— No coldness, no disdain; but as to this proud Russian, it would be easier to march an army to St. Petersburgh, and whip the Empress through a keyhole into your baggage waggon, than to subdue her petulence.

Ibra Dost thou think so? Oh, ev'ry word thou utter'd gives new ardor to my hopes, new impulses to my desires—I adore her.

Mus. Alack! alack! [with surprise].

Ibra. Oh, Mustapha, my imagination paints her till my heart grows sick with love! I see the beauteous scorner dart living lightnings from her eye, and her cheek glow with chaste disdain; I weep in anguish at her feet, I implore her compassion—Melted with my love, yet still rigid and reserv'd, I behold the bewitching conflict in her soul—I triumph in the discovery, yet conceal my delight, still implore, still complain, then seize some happy instant, when her whole soul is touch'd, and boast a victory indeed!

Mus. What then—What then, my Lord, you are not displeas'd at her haughtiness?

Ibra. Displeas'd! [smiling].

Mus. So, so, so! I have been driving on when I thought I had been pulling back; spurring a mettled courser, and neglecting the check rein [aside].

Ibra. Go on to paint her—pencil her in all her fascinating pride, deck her in the coldness which dwells on the polar Alp! My glowing soul shall burn at the description, and blaze with the fierceness of newly tasted love.

Mus. Why, as to that—to be sure as to that, she is as cold as the Alps, and all their snow-balls—the

perfectly

perfectly make's one's teeth chatter at her.—But then—

IBRA. What? [*impatiently*] then what?

Mus. Why, if truth muſt be ſpoke, there is, after all, ſomething oddiſh about her.

IBRA. Oddiſh!

Mus. Why now, my Lord, look at me—pray look at me—Ay, my Lord Baſſa, examine me well.

IBRA. To what purpoſe?

Mus. Why, the ladies of your harem ſay that this ſame beautiful Ruſſian is exceedingly like me.

IBRA. Ridiculous!

Mus. Particularly about the noſe. [Ibra. *ſhews impatience*] Nay, there are handſome likeneſſes, my Lord—I don't ſay but that ſhe may be rather hand-ſomer,

IBRA. Thou art mad.

Mus. Not that ever I ſaw the likeneſs myſelf—except ſomething in the ſhape indeed—But there I have the advantage, for her right ſhoulder, and her right ear, have too right an underſtanding, they are always together. Then her hair, to be ſure it may ſuit ſome people, but according to my fancy, the colour is execrable.

IBRA. Wretch, wert thou a chriſtian, I ſhou'd believe thee intoxicated with wine—But I'll this in-ſtant ſeek the charmer, and judge how far—[*going off*].

Enter SELIM *on the oppoſite ſide.*

SELIM. My Lord, a Meſſenger from the Divan.

IBRA. [*turns and ſtamps*] What ſay'ſt thou?

SELIM. A meſſage from the Divan with weighty diſpatches.

IBRA. I wiſh they had been *weightier*, that his ſpeed might have been leſs—Let him wait and be re-freſhed. [*ſtill going*]

SELIM. He is order'd to hurry your reply, and to return without delay to the Sublime Porte.

IBRA. Impoſſible! I ſay—I—would the Sublime Porte were ſunk beneath their own lumber. [*Exit.*

SELIM.

SELIM. What is all this? What does the wind carry now?

MUS. [*angrily*] Whims and oddities of all forts and colours—The humours of Baffas I find it is as impoffible to guefs at, as at the weight of moon-fhine.

SELIM. See! Alexina is weeping in that arbour.

MUS. Blefs her! And her cheeks through the fhining tear, look like carnations when they are firft wafhed in the dew of the morning.—Retire for a moment.   [*Exit* SELIM.

Enter ALEX. *from an Alcove.*

ALEX. O Muftapha! I have witnefs'd thy kind-nefs trembling and grateful—But, alas! what will it avail? The darknefs of night hangs upon my foul—Hope has forfaken me!

MUS. Ay, that's becaufe you did not grafp her faft—Treat Hope as you would a favourite lover, Lady! never lofe fight of it.

ALEX. Thou art light!

MUS. Even fo is hope—as light as one of your own country rein deer—and to carry on the compari-fon, it will whifk you *like* a rein-deer over all the bitter frofts of life: Buckle hope to your fledge, and you will travel over the tirefome wafte, difdaining the blaft, and fmiling at the tempeft.

ALEX. O that I could *feize* her! But how is it poffible within thefe walls? thefe walls, the temple of loofe defires, the abode of a tyrant and his flaves? Muftapha! could'ft thou effect my efcape?

MUS. There indeed, hope will give you the flip—for I could as eafily efcape into the air, and pluck a feather from the flying eagle, as help you in that, and to tell you the truth, my mafter will not much longer be dallied with.

ALEX Dreadful words! Thou canft not guefs at their weight—a tumbling rock to crufh this worthlefs frame, would not,—could not give me half the horror.

MUS. She frightens me—her eye is wild!

ALEX.

ALEX. I do swear to thee,—THEE! to whom my fruitless vows were paid, never to forget that I am thine—never to suffer the slightest violation of our sacred love.—This [*drawing a dagger*] is thy surety. To be used in that moment, when heav'n itself will approve the suicide, when applauding angels will nerve my arm to strike the blow! and this vow, I call thee, heav'n, from thy highest throne, to witness and record! [*Exit.*

MUS. By my turban, I hardly know where I stand. Women of different countries have different souls, I believe; and I am sure this is the first time this sort of soul was ever in a harem [*walks a little and considers*]. Come hither, Selim.

Enter SELIM.

MUS. Go to the Janissary Heli, he has sent me notice, that he has captured some slaves and other merchandize.—Tell him I shall be directly there, to look at his women and his velvets.

SELIM. So! then we shall have some other females, fate willing to plague us. I swear of all the merchandize our traders deal in, that of women is the most troublesome and unprofitable—And our wise and puissant Baffa is as much out in his chart of courtship, as he would be in that of the moon.—Why, he's as melancholy as a moping Spaniard on the outside of his mistress's grate.

DUETTE. SELIM and MUSTAPHA.

Deuce take whining,
Pouting, pining,
What jokes in all this pother,
If one wont do,
Nor let me woo,
I'd fit me with another.
If blue eyes frown,
I'd turn to brown,
Nor lose an hour in sighing,
Shou'd all the sex
Combine to vex,
They'd ne'er see me dying.

SCENE

SCENE *A wide Court with several unfinished*
Buildings.

[*Slaves discover'd at work at a distance. Two slaves drive barrows across the stage, and go off, followed by* A LA GREQUE.]

A LA GR. Aye, wheel away, comrades—wheel away! Hang me if *I* do though. I'll wheel no more of their rubbish. Let the Baffa dig his own dirt [*oversetting the barrow*]. Why, the sun here in Turkey seems to mind nothing but how to keep himself warm [*seating himself on the ground*]. The poets talk of his being a coachman by trade; but hang me if I don't believe he was a baker, and his oven is always hot.—I wish he'd make acquaintance with a north wind now, for half an hour, or a good strong south wester.—Lud, lud! how I do long for a wind! If I was in Lapland, I'd buy all that the witches of that country have bottled up for ten years to come [*sings*].

Blow, ye pretty little breezes,
Bustle, bustle midst the treeses.

Enter AZIM.

AZIM. How now, you lazy boar! What are you seated for, and tuning your pipes in the middle of the day?—To work—to work, sirrah!

A LA GR. Tuning my pipes! Why, I like to tune my pipes—and I don't like to work, good Mr. Muffulman—I don't indeed!

AZIM. Then you shall smart, good Mr. Christian [*shaking his whip.*]

A LA GR. What, would you take the trouble to beat me such a day as this? My dear Sir, the fatigue wou'd kill you—I can't be so unchristian as to suffer it [*Azim gives him a stroke*]. Nay, if *you* strike, [*getting up*] *I* stand.—Pray, Sir, what may be your office in this place?

3   AZIM.

Azim. To keep you and your fellow-flaves to their duty.

A la Gr. And who keeps *you* to *your* duty?

Azim. Who? why, myself to be sure.

A la Gr. Then I think yourself is a very ill-favour'd fcoundrel, to oblige you to perform a duty fo diftreffing to your politenefs.

Azim. You are an odd fifh!

A la Gr. No, I am one of a pair—I have a twin-brother juft like me.

Azim. The man who was taken with you?

A la Gr. No—he has not fuch good fortune; he's a Ruffian count, poor fellow! and was my mafter.—Gad, I could make you laugh about him.

Azim. Well!

A la Gr. About two months ago, Mr. Slave-driver, he was married.

Azim. Well!

A la Gr. A pretty girl faith, and daughter to one of our great Ruffian boyards—a boyard ranks as a marquis did in France, and as a laird ftill does in Scotland—I love to elucidate.

Azim. Well!

A la Gr. So, Sir, a few hours after the ceremony, before the fun was gone down, and before the moon had thought about dreffing herself for the evening—Whip! his pretty bride was gone.

Azim. Where?

A la Gr. That's the very thing he would get at.—Ma'am and he were walking like two doves in the boyard's garden, which garden was border'd by trees, which trees were border'd by the fea—Out fprings from the wood forty Turks with forty fabres, and forty pair of great monftrous whifkers, which fo frighten'd the bride, that inftead of running away, fhe fainted away, and ftaid there.

Azim. Hah, hah! then my countrymen had a prize.

A la Gr. That they had, worth two Jew's eyes. Six of them hurried off with her to a Felucca, which lay at the edge of the wood; and all the reft employ'd

D

my

my matter. I fuppofe they would have had him too,
but the boyard, with a large party of friends, appearing at the top of a walk, they thought fit to make off
with what they had.—Well, my matter's bridal bed
was, that night, the beach, where he ftaid raving and
beating himfelf, as tho' he took himfelf for one of the
Turkifh ravifhers.

AZIM. Ha, ha, ha! thy ftory is well—fo, all
that night he walk'd in the garden—Oh, and the
nightingales, I warrant, fung refponfes to his com-
plaints, and the melancholy wood-dove cooed in fym-
pathetic forrow.—It muft have been very pleafant.

A LA GR. O, a pleafant night as could be; but
it coft him a fortnight's lying in bed ; for a hiffing
hot fever laid hold of him ; and the doctors, with all
their rank and file of phials and boluffes, could hardly
drive him out of his veins.

AZIM. Well, now go to your labour [twirling
him round].

A LA GR. O, my dear domine, I have not finifh'd
yet.—I want to tell you how he join'd the army, to
have an opportunity of revenge, and how, in all the
fkirmifhes we have had, he has drawn more Turkifh
blood than——

AZIM. Go! you are an idle rafcal, and would
rather talk an hour than work a minute—Go, or I
will draw fome of thy French blood to balance ac-
counts with your matter.

A LA GR. Sir, you are extremely polite; the moft
getleman-like, civil, courtly, well-behav'd flave-dri-
ver I have ever had the felicity to encounter [takes up
the barrow] My fervice to your Lady, Sir ! [Azim
lafhes him off.]

AZIM. The time he mentions, about two months,
is about the period when our Felucca landed Alexina,
and his account tallies exactly with the account of the
failors—Aye, it muft be fo.—Now, would it add to
her mifery to know that her hufband is fo near her ?
I muft confider, and fhe fhall either know it, or not,
according to the effect which I think it will produce.
—I know fhe hates me, and let her look to it.

Enter

Enter ORLOFF,

My good Lord Count, pray be fo good as to take this fpade in your hand—Dig you muft, and fhall—I have had the honour to bring down as noble fpirits as yours to the grindftone before now.

ORLOFF. Inflict your punifhments! to thofe I can fubmit, but not to labour.

AZIM. Why not? Has Nature made any diftinction between you and the reft of the flaves? Look at yourfelf, Sir!—Your form, your limbs, your habit! are they in aught different from the reft?

ORLOFF. [*haughtily*] BIRTH has made a diftinction!

AZIM. That I deny—The plea of birth is of all others the moft fhadowy. There, at leaft, Nature has been ftrictly impartial: the fon of an Emprefs receives life on the fame terms with the fon of a peafant.

ORLOFF. Pride then, and Fortune, make diftinctions.

AZIM. True; but Fortune has deferted you, and pray recommend it to your pride to follow her, that you may, without trouble, attend to your bufinefs.—Here! take the fpade

ORLOFF. [*fnatches the fpade and flings it down*] There, if you dare again infult me, I'll hurl *thee* there, and tread on thee.

AZIM. Now, if the Baffa had not commanded me to be gentle to him, I would have beaten him with thongs till his broken fpirit brought him to my feet for mercy: but if I can't bend it, I'll torture it. [*afide*] So, you think to mafter me, do ye?

ORLOFF. I think not of thee.

AZIM. No, I fuppofe—Ha, ha!—I fuppofe your pretty wife is——

ORLOFF. My wife—my wife—Oh, art thou appriz'd that I had a wife? [AZIM *grins*] Oh! fpeak to me, tell me if thou know'ft her—Nay, turn not from me!—All the lineaments of thy face become

D 2   important

important—if thou wilt not speak to me, let me gaze on *them*, and there gather my fate.

AZIM.   Well, gaze and gaze! Can't thou there read her story? Dost thou know *whether* she breathes, and *where?* Dost thou behold thy lovely wife triumphant in a seraglio, or submissive in a bathing house?

ORLOFF. Oh, villain! monster! neither. By every glittering star in heaven, if she lives, she's chaste! [*pauses and strikes his forehead*]   Had I gold and jewels, I would pour the treasure at thy feet, but now have mercy on me—Oh, I beseech thee, tell me if Alexina lives.

AZIM.   Ha, ha, ha! if Alexina lives! [*laughs again, then walks slowly off.*]

ORLOFF.   Nay, thou shalt not avoid me—I will pursue thee, kneel at thy feet, perform the most menial offices, so thou wilt tell me of my Alexina!

AZIM.   [*turning*] Now, where are the distinctions of thy birth? Do they prevent thy feeling like the vulgarest son of Nature?

ORLOFF.   Thou shalt chide long, if thou wilt at length soften the anguish of my soul—Oh, hear me, hear me!   [*Follows him out.*

END OF THE SECOND ACT.

A C T III.

SCENE I. *The Garden.*

Enter MUSTAPHA.

COME along, I say—Why, what do you stand there for?—O the difference of women! This is a stubborn one, I warrant her—Though she saw me pay down the money for her, she has not the least notion that she's a slave—Well, if you won't come, Madam, I'll fetch ye.—[*Goes out and re-enters with* PAULINA, *new-dress'd.*]

PAU. Law! how you hawl one—I tell ye, I don't like to walk here—Let me alone. [*Trying to disengage her hand.*].

MUS. Come, come, Madam, none of your airs—You must here be obedient and civil—Come along. The Janissary of whom I bought you, told me you was a good natured, complaisant creature.

PAU. Yes, but he was not so rough as you are; he made me throw away my peasant weeds, and gave me all these fine cloaths. See this tiffany, all spotted with silver; look at this beautiful turban—He gave it me all!

MUS. Why, that was only to set off your beauty, that you might fetch a better price; but I bought you for your good humour only. Here is a sweet woman who pines and sighs till she puts one in mind of a myrtle blossom, all palenets and fragrance.

PAU. [*with quickness*] What's that to I? I suppose I shall be pale and flagrant too, if I am to be kept down by you.

MUS. Who wants to keep you down? Behave yourself prettily, and you may live as merrily here as sparrows upon a may-bush. The gentle creature for

D 3

whom I bought ye, is your countrywoman, and I
guefs'd you might divert her with your *fenfible*
prattle.

PAU. Ah, did you fo? Why, you guefs'd as tho'
it was your trade then—for I am the moft divertingeft
creature in our whole village, and if I could but fee
my father, and brother Peter—

Mus. Well, if you behave difcreetly—I'll buy
your father, and brother Peter—

PAU. Buy! buy! Why, you talk of buying us,
as though we were bafkets of eggs, or bales of cotton.

Mus. Yes, it is the mode here—Every country
has its fancies, and we are fo fond of liberty, that we
always buy it up as a rarity.

PAU. What, did you buy all thofe ugly men that
I fee at work yonder?

Mus. Men! Make no miftakes, child—It would
be death for a man to be feen here. None ever venture a foot within thefe fhades.

PAU. No! why then do *you* venture here?

Mus. O, as for me, I—I—hold your tongue,
[*angrily*] and make no impertinent inquiries.

PAU. But I *will* make inquiries. What do all
them there ugly men do here, I fay?

Mus. Why them there ugly men were bought to
keep you pretty women in order.

PAU. In order! Why what controul have they
over us?

Mus. Oh, they are guards and fpies; and are now
and then convenient at taking off a lady's head, or
fuiting her neck with a bowftring, when the whim
happens to feize a great man, of amufing his feraglio
with a tragic gala.

PAU. Why, what wicked wretches you all are,
then! Get out of my fight, do! You look fo ugly I
can't bear ye, and if I was a great man, I'd ftring you
all together upon a rope that fhou'd reach from here
to Saint Peterfburgh.

Mus. Ah, you have a fpirit, I fee—Hark ye,
huffey [*feizes her arm.*]

PAU.

Pau. O, dear heart, do not look fo ferocious! I really believe you are a female tyger.

Mus. Dread my claws then! See, here is the gentle creature for whom I bought thee—had fhe had thy impertinence, fhe might have pined in folicude for me.

Enter Alexina, [*Hastily.*]

Alex. Nay, but it is—Impoffible! And yet it is fo! Art thou not Paulina, the daughter of my father's vaffal, Petrowitz?—Alas! thou art. Unhappy girl! what——

Pau. Goodnefs, goodnefs! If it is not the Lady Alexina, may I be whipt!

Alex. Dear Paulina, what dreadful deftiny brought thee hither?

Pau. Deftiny do you call him? [*looking at Muſta-pha*] Why, this place is all full of dreadful deftinies, I think. Some with black whifkers, and fome with grey ones. Was it this little odd deftiny who bought you too?

Alex. Alas! thy queftion brings back fuch a rufh of forrows—Oh! thou can'ft not be ignorant that I was torn from my hufband within the very hour that made me his, [*weeps*] and dragg'd from blifs to flavery.

Pau. I did not know that you was *here*—but I am monftrous glad to meet you here—It is the luckieft thing—I have always been in luck!

Mus. Yes, that compliment is a proof of it. You are vaftly lucky there! Well, go on, and amufe her, child—I fhall enlarge your party prefently. [*Goes out.*]

Pau. The little body is as pert as though it was five feet high—But, for all him, I will fay, my dear lady, that I would not but have feen you here for the beft gown I have—Not even for this, though it is fo fine.

Alex. Hah, Paulina! I fear that this drefs is the mark of thy difhonour—I fear thou art undone!

Pau.

PAU. Undone indeed! I think we are both undone ; to be brought into such an odd, out-of-the-way
country as this—ha, ha, ha, ha. I have been here
but an hour, and it seems an hundred—In one place a
parcel of copper-colour creatures, without tongues,
pop out, glaring with their saucer eyes, and if you
want to talk and be a little sociable, ba, ba, ba, is all
you can get—I believe they learnt their alphabet of
the sheep—Then in another corner—

ALEX [*impatiently*] Pray reserve your observa-
tions—I have questions to ask, which tear my heart-
strings to pronounce—Speak to me of Orloff—Oh,
my Orloff! Speak to me of my parents.—Did they
support the moment which dragg'd me from them ?

PAU. Truly as bad as you cou'd wish —At last
't was said that my Lord, the Count, went into the
army, and there he has play'd about him valiantly! I
warrant he'll pay the Turks for robbing him of you,
though, may be, they won't like his coin.

ALEX. Oh, preserve him THOU, in whose hand
remains the fate of battles!

Enter MUSTAPHA, *with* LAURETTA.

MUS. Here, I have brought ye Lauretta ; she is
a girl of enterprise, and I have a fancy which her in-
triguing spirit will bring to perfection.

ALEX. Alas! how can she serve me? Can she
restore me to my country—to my husband— ?

MUS. Fear her not—she has as many plots as
dimples; so I leave ye together —Stand on one side.
[*To Pau. who is in his way.*]

PAU. Aye, on any side but your's, Mr. Destiny
[*crosses.*]—I hope you and I shall be always at contrary
sides.

MUS. So hope I, Miss Nimble Tongue! For if
you were always beside me, I should soon be beside
myself. [*Exit.*

LAUR. Dear madam, look a little cheerfully—I.
have a thought in my head—Hark ye, my dear [*to*
Paulina].

Paulina]—you are a Ruffian, I find—What fort of lovers do your countrymen make?

PAU. How fhould I know? I never had but three —One was old enough to be my.father, fo, I ufed to kneel down and afk his blefling—So, one day, he gave me a curfe, and walked off.—The next was a fchoolmafter, and he had fuch a trick of correction, that, had I married him, I fhould have been in conftant fear of the birch.—The third was a foldier—but as I neither liked to follow the camp, nor to live a widow bewitch'd, I made him beat his march.

LAUR. Brava! you difpos'd of them all like a girl of fpirit, and yet, I think, had the cafe been mine, I fhould have taken a march with the foldier—I do love foldiers.—A regiment on its march always makes my heart fhiver to pieces amongft a thoufand Cæfars and Alexanders. [*To Alexina*] Has the Baffa feen you yet?

ALEX. He fent by Muley to command me to his prefence, but I will firft rufh into the arms of death.

LAUR. Ha, ha, ha! fuch a refolution in this country! Rather rufh into the arms of death, than into the arms of a handfome lover! the notion is exotic—it is an ice plant of the North—and our hot fun will wither its honours, depend on't.

ALEX. [*Scornfully.*] Are you the friend who was to foothe my forrows? Alas! where fhall HONOUR be *honour'd*, if the mouth of WOMAN caft on its contempt!

LAUR. Ah, pardon my levity, for I mean to ferve you.

ALEX. In *you*, the contented inhabitant of a feraglio, fuch a profanation may be pardon'd; but alas! in the world, the grace of chaftity is fcarcely longer acknowledged! I have heard the wife and the daughter affix ridicule to the name. O virtue! where canft thou expect worfhip, when the fpeech of the matron and the virgin *unhallows* thy facred idea?

LAUR. I am not fo loft, but I can feel and *thank* you for your reproof; and as the firft fruits of it, I will labour for your efcape from a fituation, which,

to you, muft be mifery indeed! But, madam, we muft
confer alone—I intreat you to retire with me.

ALEX. Alas! fo miferable is my fituation, that I
am obliged to accept fervices from thofe whom the
feelings of my heart wou'd knpel me to fhun.

[*Exit.*

LAUR. [*To Paulina, who is following.*] Ah!
not fo quick, mifs! Do you ftay here 'till I return—
Stir nor, I charge you.   [*Exit.*

PAU. Stay here, indeed! There is pretty good
care taken that one fhou'dn't run away. The walls
are as high as a cathedral, and fuch frightful looking
oddities prowling about, that a moufe could not run
from one fhrub to another without obfervation—
How they all ftare at me! So! there's another of
them—He looks rather better than the reft—but I
fhall have nothing to fay to him. [*Regards her drefs,
&c.*]

Enter IBRAHIM, *followed by flaves. He turns and
fpeaks to them with impatience.*

IBRA. No more, no more of bufinefs. Let not a
thought of public duty here obtrude itfelf—I have
already facrificed thofe hours to it, due to a dearer
caufe. [*The flaves retire.*] And now for my reward! Now will I feek the charming obdurate, nor
ever leave—Hah! fhe is there! The lovely fugitive—
I have found her—I have found her!

PAU. Heigho! what fhall I do with myfelf! I'll
gather flowers for lady Alexina.

IBRA. Yes, fhe has a thoufand charms, and my
heart is already in her chains.—How dared Muftapha
deceive me? He talked of deformity—her form is
fymmetry itfelf, and her hair which he decried, is fit
for the bow-ftrings of the god of love.

PAU. Hang this fharp thorn, it has made my
finger bleed.

IBRA. [*Advancing.*] But you, charming Ruffian!
ftill more barbarous, are born to make hearts bleed.
[PAU. *looks at him attentively, then toffes her head
scornfully*

fornfully away.] What a true picture they have given me of her scorn! Will you not speak to me?

PAU. [*Looks at him again.*] I wonder at some people.

IBRA. What dost thou say? Oh, that mouth is too lovely to be closed so soon.

PAU. [*Talking to her flowers.*] You are very pretty, and you are very sweet, but you are not complete yet—Good Mr. What-d ye-call—reach me that flower that grows so high.

IBRA. With transport! [*presents the flower.*] shall I arrange them for you?

PAU. Get along, do!

IBRA. Teach me to do something that may not displease you.

PAU. Get out of my way, I say.

IBRA. Do you know me?

PAU. Not I, nor never desire to know ye—I wish I was out of this wretched place altogether, I know that.

IBRA. It shall be the business of my life to make you happy in it.

PAU. You! ha, ha, ha.

IBRA. You are surely unacquainted with my rank, and my fituation.

PAU. No, no—I know that.—Do hold your non-sense.

IBRA. [*With displeasure.*] Your haughtiness I was prepared to bow to, but I knew not how to meet your contempt.

PAU. Don't begin to redden at me—I mind ye no more than I do this fallow leaf—There—see—I blow it, and away it flies—go after it—there lies your way.

IBRA. But not the attraction—You bid me go, whilst your eyes chain me here.

PAU. Then I'll shut them—There—now how do you like me?

IBRA. In vain you shut your eyes, unless you cou'd likewise hide that rofy mouth, those teeth, those features, that form! I could love you though you were blind.

PAU.

PAU. Love! What, can you love? Such a hard-hearted—*Turkifh*—creature as you love?

IBRA. Can I? yes, to diftraction! It is not poffible for me to tell you *how* I could adore you— Whole days wou'd be loft in gazing on your charms! I could hang on your breath like the humming-bird on the vapour of the rofe, and I fhould drink your glances, 'till my foul, fick with excefs of pleafure, would leave me fcarce power to murmur forth my blifs.

PAU. Now, what can he mean by all that? I believe a bifhop could not talk finer! [*Afide*] I tell ye what, mifter, you may make grand fpeeches about this and that; but I hate both you and your love; and if ever you teize me with it any more, I'll make you repent, that I will [*fings*].

SONG. PAULINA.

You think to talk of this and that,
And keep me here in filly chat,
　　But I know, I know better.
There clearly lies, kind Sir, your way,
Purfue it then I humbly pray,
　　And me you'll make your debtor.

Why, blefs my ftars, it's very odd,
That here upon this harmlefs fod,
　　I cannot ftay in quiet.
But now you know fo clear my mind,
Mayhap you'll leave me here behind,
　　The path feems wide, pray try it.

IBRA. Charming fongftrefs!—I dare not purfue her.—How well fhe knows the power of love, to treat with difdain the man in whofe hands is her fate! Hah! would I fuffer her thus to leave me, but that at laft fhe *muft* be mine! Go then, lovely tyrant, indulge thy fcorn, and treat me like an humble flave— A moment comes when thou fhalt repay me! [*Exit.*

PAU. [*Coming down*] So! he's gone!

Enter

Enter ALEXINA, MUSTAPHA, *and* LAURETTA.

LAUR. Hah! fee what fweet flowers I have gather'd for you! Why did you ftay fo long?

ALEX. Oh, let me embrace thee!

PAU. What, all this for the flowers?

ALEX. No, for hope—for foft returning hope!
Paulina, the powerful Baffa is thy flave—He loves
thee—I have witneffed your interview, and blefs that
fortune which has done for me in an inftant, what, by
a train of artifices, we meant to have procured.

MUS. Ah, but, you little rogues, 'tis I that have
done it, 'tis I that have brought about all this, though
like fome other great actions, more is owing to chance
than fkill.

PAU. Why, what have *you* done to be fo full of
your brags?

LAUR. What, are you not fenfible of your happinefs? To have fubdued the heart of one of the
hand-fomeft, and moft powerful men in the empire?

PAU. Men!—What are you talking about?—Oh
then, that handfome man is not one of thofe odious
creatures who bowftring us? Laws! how could I treat
the gentleman fo? I'll run after him, and make it
up. [*running off*]

ALEX. [*following and holding her*] Stay! or you
undo me.

PAU. Well then, the next time I fee him, I'll tell
him that I'm afham'd of myfelf; and I'll try by all
due civilities to appeafe his anger.

ALEX. Oh, not for worlds—Still you will undo
me, my fate is in your hands.

MUS. Hark ye, my pretty maid, our Baffa, like
all great men, has his fancies, he does not like too
much honey on his bread.

PAU. Laws! Ha, ha, ha!

LAUR. If you wifh to retain his heart, you muft
p'ague it—if you are tender you'll lofe him.

PAU. Why, that's the way in my country too; as
foon as our ladies grow fond, their lovers grow cold;
for all the world like the little Dutch painted man

E   and

and woman in the weather box, when one pops out, the other pops in—never in a mind.

Mus. Keep the leſſon in *your* mind, and you may be a great lady—only take care not to begin your pops too ſoon. You ſee ſhe is apt.

Laur. O, as a parrot! Come, my good girl, you ſhall go to my chamber, and I will give you the prettieſt leſſon you ever yet learnt—I'll teach you in half an hour all the arts of a fine lady, and you ſhall be able to play on your lover as you wou'd on an harpſichord. The whole gamut of his mind ſhall be in your poſſeſſion, and every note of it obedient to your wiſh.

Alex. Be attentive to her leſſons, my dear Paulina; perhaps my honour, and my felicity, depend on your ſucceſs—O preſerve your own innocence, and be the guardian of mine!

Pau. Preſerve my own innocence! Ay, to be ſure I will—for my father has read to me in many a good book, which ſays, that a woman, when ſhe loſes her innocence, loſes her charms, and that, like a faded roſe dropt from the tree, the foot of every paſſenger will tread on her in her decay. O, who would loſe their innocence! My dear lady, why, your eyes look as bright again as they did when I fiſt ſaw you.

Alex. It is becauſe Hope hath ſhed its luſtre on them. [Laur. *leads off* Paulina.] My heart is full; my veins confeſs a warmer flow, and the brighteſt viſions glides before me. O, nature! thou who haſt made us capable of ſo much bliſs, why is it thy decree that we ſhall ſink in ſorrow? Why muſt our joys be ſo often ſhrivel'd by the cold touch of indurating DESPAIR!   [*Exit.*

Enter Selim *and* Fatima.

Fat. Selim, was not that the Ruſſian ſlave who departed as we enter'd? Surely it was, and with a look of pleaſure!—

Selim. Pleaſure! I am glad to hear it. I am ſure her melancholy has thrown a gloom over the whole harem.

Fat.

FAT. What an odd whim it is in our master to grow fond of the *mind* of a woman! Did ever any body hear of a woman's *mind* before as an object of passion?

SELIM. I don't understand it.

DUETTE. SELIM *and* FATIMA.

Give me (you) a female soft and kind,
　　Whose joy 'twould be to please me (ye);
'The beauties of her precious mind,
　　Would neither charm nor seize me (ye).

The dimpled cheek, and sparkling eye,
　　To me (you) are wit and sound sense;
And better worth a lover's sigh,
　　Than stores of mental nonsense.

'The touch of honied velvet lips
　　Is reason and bright science,
And he who at that fountain dips,
　　May scorn the *Nine*'s alliance.

END OF THE THIRD ACT.

ACT

A C T IV.

SCENE I.—*A Quadrangle—On one Side of the Square is a very high Garden Wall; behind which are heard frequent Bursts of Laughter——*A LA GREQUE *is seen moving from Place to Place, trying to peep through.*

A LA GREQUE.

DEVIL take the workmen who built the wall! Not a chink or cranny can I find to send in the thousardth part of an eye-beam [*laugh within*]. There they go again! Oh, you sweet tits you! I wish I was one amongst ye. [*Enter a Turk and crosses*] Hark ye, Mr. Gravity! Is there no getting a peep at these jolly girls?

TURK. No.

A LA GR. What, are they never suffer'd to be seen by a handsome Christian young fellow like me?

TURK. No.

A LA GR. D'ye think they'd take it amiss if a man was to venture his neck over the wall, to get at them?

TURK. No.

A LA GR. D'ye believe the Bassa would forgive such an innocent piece of curiosity?

TURK. No.

A LA GR. Egad, you manage your words discreetly—Are you afraid your flock won't last the winter, shou'd you spend too many these summer months?

TURK. No.

A LA GR. Well done, my boy! Since you are so fond of the word, I'll give ye a song on the subject.

SONG,

SONG, A la Greque.

A pretty gemman once I faw.
The neighbours faid he ftudied law,
 When full of grief,
 In 's hand a brief,
  A poor man came,
 Good Sir, he cried,
 Plead on my fide,
  The lawyer *carelefs* anfwer'd—No !

A rich gown'd parfon wou'd you afk
To do a charitable tafk
 For Tom and Sue,
 A couple true,
  Who'd fain be tied,
 With eye elate,
 And ftrut of ftate,
  The parfon *furly* anfwers—No !

Should lab'ring honeft low-fed Dick,
In fpite of ftarving, very fick
 To doctor fend,
 By fome kind friend
  To *beg* advice ;
 He ftraight will fee
 No hope of fee,
And ten to one he anfwers—No !

A Tenator you afk'd to vote,
The dear red book he knows by rote,
 His country's good
 He underftood
  You had in view,
 But fhou'd he find
 No place defign'd,
His bow *polite* you know, means—No !

To a young beauty wou'd you kneel,
And talk of all the pangs you feel?
        With eye afkance
        She'll fteal a glance,
            And blufhing figh,
        But fhou'd you prefs
        Her power to blefs,
She'll whifper forth a *trembling*—No!

TURK.   I like your fong.
A LA GR.   I like your praife.
TURK.   And to reward ye, I'll fhew ye a place,
where, by the lelp of loofe bricks, and good climbing,
I fometimes get a fquint at the girls;—though if it
was known, I fhould never fquint on this fide paradife
again.
A LA GR.   You are an honeft fellow, and 'tis pity
you are a Turk—but it can't be help'd, and 'tis to be
hoped a man may travel to heaven at laft, though he
never leaves the country in which he was fwaddled.
—Come along!   [*hurries him off*]

SCENE II. *The Garden.*

*Enter female Slaves, finging and beckoning to their
companions, who enter from oppofite wings all the
way up. During the fong others enter, dancing
to the mufic.*

CHORUS—OF FEMALE SLAVES.

Come away! come away!
    Companions fo gay!
Come away! Come away!
    Companions fo gay! &c.

SONG, AND CHORUS.

This is Freedom's precious hour,
    Welcome, airy, fportive Mirth!
We'll enjoy thee whilft we've pow'r,
    Give to all thy whimfies birth.

Let

Let the crofs ones burft with fpite,
　　We'll ne'er heed their fhrugs or frowns,
Vary ev'ry fweet delight,
　　While blythe Joy our labour crowns.

CHORUS.

Come away! &c.

A LA GR. *[from the top of the wall]* Hah! hah!
you little merry rogues, you're there, are ye?
　　[The women fhriek, and all go off, except LAUR.
　　and FATIMA.

LAUR. What audacity! Prefuming flave, do you
know the confequence of your temerity?

A LA GR. Yes, I can guefs at it, that you are all
fet a longing, and are ready to afk me to come down
amongft you.

LAUR. You are impertinent.   *[Exit.*

FAT. Do you hear, young man?—" you are impertinent"—Yes, you are an infolent, prefuming, au-
dacious—fweet fellow, hang me if he is not. *[Exit.*

A LA GR. Ah, you fweet little faucy jade, come
under the wall, and blow me a kifs—You won't!
Why get along then, you ill-humour'd baggages—
Hah! what, you look back, do you? You'd better
think on't, and turn—What, the grapes are four, are
they? Ah, ah! I underftand you—this is a fine place
for the gypfies, hang me if it is not—Thefe Turks
have a life on't—Such fine girls, and fuch fine gardens
—Whu! who comes here? This is another—Yes,
yes, I'll turn Turk—There's nothing like it, I fee.

Enter PAULINA.

A LA GR. Hark ye, pretty maid—come this
way.

PAU. Gracious! where can that voice come
from? I fee nobody. *[running about]*

A LA GR. I fay, you little rogue, if—Why, how
can this be? If my eyes are my own eyes, and if her
　　　　　　　　　　　　　　　　　　　　eyes

eyes are hers, it is Paulina, the daughter of old Petrowitz.

PAU. [*Clapping her hands.*]   As sure as that impudent head was once on the shoulders of A la Greque; who ever thought of seeing it on the top of a
Turkish wall? How came you amongst them? Did
they buy you too?

A LA GR.   Buy me! No, I was taken fighting in
a little skirmish, where I had only time to disarm half
a dozen Turks, and kill a few Bassas; and now the
cowardly rogues have shut me up here, for fear I
should do them further mischief—I believe they think
I have a design upon the crown.

PAU.   Law! only think of it.

A LA GR.   Didn't you hear that the Grand Turk
had offer'd a reward for my head?

PAU.   Your head!—Why, what could he do with
it?

A LA GR.   Faith, I had no inclination to inquire,
so I took to my heels and carried it off.

PAU.   Then how came it there? [*pointing.*]

A LA GR.   Didn't I tell ye that a whole army set
upon me and my master, and brought us——

PAU.   Mercy! is your master here, count Orloff?

A LA GR.   Is he? aye, lock'd up within the brazen
gates of this——

PAU.   Why, if ever I heard the like—Within the
same gates is locked up lady Alexina, who was stole
from him by these odious Turks.

A LA GR.   She here too! Why, this place is like
the sick lion's den, where all the beasts of the forest
assembled together.

Voices [*without*] Help! help! here's a man talking to one of the female slaves.

A LA GR.   I'll prove ye a liar in your teeth [*goes
down*].

SLAVES *enter.*

ISM.   Where is the man to whom you talked?

PAU   Man!—Do men grow on the bushes in your
country? There is no other way of a man's finding
himself in this garden, I fancy.

ISM

Ism. I heard his voice—Let us drag her before the Baſſa.—·Go you and ſearch the gardens.

2. Slave, [Apart] Take care what ye do—This is the new ſlave whom we were commanded to treat with ſo much reſpect—We ſhall bring miſchief on ourſelves—Her word will go further than ours as long as ſhe's in favour.

Ism. I underſtand you —[turning]—I thought I heard the voice of a man,—but ſounds deceive one—it might be a bulfinch perhaps—beg pardon for the miſtake, lady.   [Exeunt Slaves.

Pau. A man a bullfinch, ha, ha, ha! Theſe ſtupid creatures might be perſuaded, I dare ſay, that a cat was a green ſlipper. Well, how oddly things turn out!—Little does lady Alexina think her huſband is ſo near her.—Hiſt! A la Greque! A la Greque!—[Looking towards the top of the wall]—Ha! he's gone now—Well, I'll run and bleſs her with the news, and then take one more leſſon for my behaviour to the Baſſa.—I ſhall be able, after that, to behave as proudly as though my father were a noble of the land—Let me ſee—How is it to be a fine lady? Firſt, I muſt diſguiſe all the feelings of my heart—But how can I do ſo without telling fibs? Well, fine ladies don't mind that.—Second, when he kneels, I muſt turn from him, or hum a tune—thus—[hums]—Did you ſpeak to me, Sir?—And when the charming man—O Lord! I ſhall never do it, as though I were us'd to it—When he attempts to kiſs me, I muſt complain of his inſolence, and walk away in this manner. [Walks off ſcornfully.]

SCENE, The Buildings.

Enter Azim, with other Slaves.

Azim. Shall we ſtand by each other, brothers? Will you be faithful?

Ism. Aye, that we will; we muſt do as you bid us—You are over us. By allowing that, we generally come over him. [To another.]

Azim.

AZIM. Well then, you fee how the cafe ftands; fhe is come wonderfully into favour, and will, with-out doubt, be reveng'd on us, for the feverities fhe receiv'd in our lord's abfence. The Baffa has juft now threaten'd vengeance to all who difpleafe her.

SLAVE. Will it not difpleafe her then to be put into a prifon?

AZIM. 'Tis likely it may—but what is that to us? We can, whenever we determine to do fo, connive at her efcape; and if we allow her to leave the palace, fhe'll readily pardon the prifon; fo, fhe'll be gratified, and we fhall be fkreen'd.

ISM. Well, well; let her be locked up as you faid, and then perfuade him fhe has efcaped.

2d. SLAVE. We can dig down part of an old wall, and drop a ladder at the bottom, and then it won't be doubted.

AZIM. Yes; and that old tower will be a proper place to confine her in; then, if need be, fhe can hereafter be produced, for I don't entirely approve of poifoning her.

ISM. No, not at prefent—it may be more con-venient hereafter—[drily]—Where fhall we feize her?

AZIM. She is generally in the garden, and alone —it will not be difficult if we watch for a moment when Muftapha is abfent.

SLAVE. Here's fome one coming

AZIM. Then let us difperfe feveral ways. People who have a plot in hand fhould never be feen together —A flight of crows always proclaims a carcafe.

[Exeunt feverally.

Enter ORLOFF *followed by* A LA GRECQUE.

ORLOFF. Purfue me not, thou contemptible wretch! My forrows are too profound to be inter-rupted by refentment at thy folly—Oh, moft inhuman fate! To know that my Alexina lives, to know that fhe exifts in this province, and not to know *where*— My chains are become heavy indeed!—They are in-fupportable!

A LA

A la Gr. Let me lift them for you, Sir—I can make them jingle lighter.

Orloff. Begone, I say.

A la Gr. Well, I'll go—People often drive their good fortune from them, like you. I shall only say, as I was saying before, that this house has a garden, and that this garden has a wall.

Orloff. Oh, my charming bride! could I but cheer thee by my voice, could I but lessen *thy* anguish, by speaking to thee *my own*.

A la Gr. Well, a *wall*—What is a *wall* to me?

Orloff. Could I, each morning, when I greet its rays, behold but thee, I could bear to live even in this wretched state, and every heavy night I could creep to my straw pallet with less despondency, having first received from thy sweet eyes, farewell!

A la Gr. To be sure the wall is a high wall, and a strong wall; but it is *but* a wall.

Orloff. If thou darest mention the wall again.

A la Gr. Well, I won't then; but was I to tell you, my Lord, what that wall contains, I really believe you'd forgive all my sauciness for ten years to come.

Orloff. Surely thou hast a meaning! What would'st thou say?

A la Gr. A meaning! Aye, such a meaning!

Orloff. Oh, trifle not!

A la Gr. Why then, in two words, I have climbed the garden wall, and who do you think I saw in the garden—Who do you think?

Orloff. Oh speak! [*grasping his hand*] Speak! my soul hangs upon thy words—Could'st thou but know what I feel!

A la Gr. Then, my Lord, there, as sure as you lost your bride on the day of marriage, there I saw the fair Paulina, daughter of old Petrowitz.

Orloff. Oh! [*drops*]

A la Gr. Mon Dieu! if the joy of that has been too much for him, how would he have borne it, if I had seen his wife? [*goes to him*] My Lord—my Lord!

I   Why

Why he's as pale as death—I dare not tell him now that Alexina is within a hundred yards of him.

ORLOFF. Bitter, bitter disappointment! it has been a stab to my heart—Barbarous wretch! [*rising and seizing him*] to raise and feed my hopes with such artful cruelty, and then—but why do I talk to thee? [*Exit.*

A LA GR. So! what he is *disappointed* then! Why if he would but have had patience, I was just going to tell him that his wife—but hang patience! 'tis a scurvy virtue, and not fit for a gentleman. *I* have no patience to know there are so many fine girls caged up here for that *greedy* Dog the Baffa. I'll try to pick a bone with him, though;—and if I can once lay hold of one of his pullets, he shall find it as difficult to get her out of my fangs, as it would be to make a judge dance, or a bishop cut capers. [*Exit.*

SCENE, *The Prison.*

[*Voices are heard without, ALEXINA shrieks.*]

AZIM. [*entering*] Stop her mouth, and drag her in. [ALEXINA *is dragg'd in—her hair dishevell'd.*]

ALEX. Monsters! if ye are of the human race, desist—O drag me not from day, and from my husband!

AZIM. This is your habitation, Madam, make the best of it.

ALEX. At whose command is it my habitation? What is my crime? You act without the knowledge of your Lord—and if you do, doubt not his vengeance! O, it is not possible that he can authorize this cruelty!

AZIM. Come, come, Madam, a few weeks spent here will quiet you a little—Your sorrows won't be half so violent a fortnight hence as they are now—Let that comfort you.

ALEX. A fortnight! Oh, it is an eternity! Death is nothing to this. Dragg'd at *such* a moment from light, and health, and hope! [*running wildly about*] O, Azim, my HUSBAND is here—my HUSBAND is at hand!

AZIM.

Azim. Then let him get ye out, if he can.

Alex. O, beſt of men, hear me! [*kneeling*] Tell him only that his Alexina is here, that he may walk round my priſon, that I may hear his ſteps through the chinks of theſe diſmal walls, and my ſoul ſhall bleſs thee.

Azim. Oh, you are mighty humble now; yet you know what infolence I have borne from you.

Alex. I meant it not—Oh, forgive me, forgive me! Here, take this ring, let it *purchaſe* my forgiveneſs. [*riſing*] It is rich, but not half ſo rich as ſhall be thy reward, if thou wilt be my friend—if thou wilt pity me!

Azim. Well, I am ſo far ſoften'd that I permit thee to uſe the apartment next to this—It has more air and light—I'll unlock it—its laſt inhabitant had it fourteen years. [*whilſt he goes to unlock it,* Alexina *claſps her hands, and fixes her eyes wildly*] There! you ſhall each 'day have your allowance of food regularly brought; but whether you are ever releaſed or not, depends on yourſelf—Be patient! That only can ſerve you.

Alex. Patient! Oh yes, I'll try to be patient, though much I fear my brain will be diſturbed.

Azim. Well, you'll be diſturbed by nothing elſe —Your apartment will be quiet enough, whatever your brain may be—Come, Madam. [*Puts her in, and ſhuts the door.*] There, ſhe's ſafe, and that makes us ſafe.—Now, let us go and fix the rope-ladder, and then ſwear ſhe has eſcaped. Comrades! They talk of countries, where, what we have done, might be puniſhed by the law—but we fear no puniſhment while we can deceive our maſter. [*Exeunt, laughing.*

END OF THE FOURTH ACT.

F   A C T

A C T V.

S C E N E,

A spacious Apartment in the Harem.

Enter PAULINA, *running from the Top.*

PAU. [*Looking back.*] THE sweet man follows
me still. Hah! Lauretta little thinks the difficulty
I have had to behave to him as tho' I hated him—
How hard it is when one sees a great gentleman, and
so handsome withal, ready to die at one's feet, to be
forced to be snappish and ill-natur'd—Laws! he's
coming here—Which way shall I run next? [*Looking
about.*]

IBRA. [*Entering*] Oh, fly me not—yet fly!
Even the distance you throw me at gives you a thousand charms, and whilst it tortures, it bewitches me.

PAU. [*Aside*] I do like to hear him talk.

IBRA. You smile! Ah, did you know the value
of those rosy smiles, you would not bestow on me
more than one in a thousand hours—Each is worth a
diadem.

PAU. I suppose you hope by all this to make me
forget I am a captive, and a slave [*pretending to cry,
then turning away, laughing.*]

IBRA. You can be neither—It is I who am *your*
slave—You hold the chains of my destiny—Ha! let
me catch your tears!

PAU. I tell you once again, that I can never be
happy here—I hate the life people lead in harems—
All is dismal, not even a window to the street! No-

2   thing

thing to look at but trees, and fountains, and great whiskers, and black slaves.

IBRA. Could I but have the transport to touch your heart, all those objects would give you new impreflions—This hated harem would feem transform'd, and would become an enchanted place of pleasure.

PAU. But I tell you, I will *never* fuffer my heart to be touch'd.—It is very hard that I muft belie my confcience fo, my heart leaps every time I look at him. [*Afide*]

IBRA. Who knows what perfevering, conftant love may do? You may at length be foften'd, at length—Oh rapture! confefs the delicious pain!

PAU. [*Afide.*] I long to confefs it now, if I might fpeak out.

IBRA. Moft charming creature, deign but to look on me, fay only that I am not hateful to you

PAU. Aye, that would be the trueft word I ever fpoke [*afide*]. But I will fay that you *are* hateful to me, and I do declare; if you ever fpeak to me about love again—I—I don't know what may be the confequence—I muft get away, or all my fine leffons will be forgot [*afide*]. In that room yonder I fee ladies finging and playing; but don't you come to us now, I charge you—I will not have you come, or if you do come in half an hour, not a word [*looking back*]— No, not one word about love. [*Exit.*

IBRA. Oh, if there is language in eyes, her words are falfe—Her lips forbid my love, but her eye invites it—Charming fex! who know how to make refufal blifs; and who can give delight even in denying! *Half an hour* did fhe banifh me—Oh, I'll follow her inftantly—Every moment fpent where fhe is not, is a moment not to be counted in my exiftence. [*Going —Noife behind.*] Ha! what noife is that? [*Puts his hand to his fcymeter.*] The founds of violence in the bofom of my retirement!

ORLOFF. [*Without.*] Bafe flaves, in vain you oppofe me! Were your mafter furrounded by inftruments of torture, and minifters of vengeance, I would force my way.

F 2 [*Forcing*

[Forcing in, Slaves endeavouring to withhold him—after them, MULEY *enters.*

IBRA. [*Fiercely.*]   Your way! What, here? Those apartments, christian, are sacred; and did not I pay some regard to your fame as a soldier, and your rank in the Imperial army, by Mahomet, your life's quick stream should pay me for the insult.

ORLOFF.   Talk not of life, dishonourable man! Restore to me my bride—Restore—but canst thou restore her? Oh, canst thou restore to me the SPOTLESS angel, whom heaven's most sacred ordinance made mine?

IBRA.   Wretches! allow a madman to invade my retirement.

ORLOFF.   Thy retirement! Thy *life*, base Turk! shall be invaded.   No madman, but an injur'd husband stands before thee! Restore her!—Give her back to me chaste as that morn, when trembling, blushing from the altar, I led her to parental fields—That morn unblest.

IBRA.   Slaves! speak, declare whom 'tis he means, or dread my vengeance—A fear hath seiz'd my soul, that curdles all my blood—Should it be so—speak! [*Furiously.*]

MULEY.   Mighty Bassa! We fear he means the lovely Russian, who adorns your harem.

IBRA.   Ah! [*wildly*] Is she his *wife?* Christian, art thou the *husband* of the beauteous slave I love?

ORLOFF.   Love! Dar'st thou give birth to such a phrase? Love! Oh that the words had scorpion's teeth to tear the throat which utters them!

IBRA.   And art thou—O curst discovery! It is too true—My heart tells me it is true, and hates thee for the conviction.   Tear him from my presence—I dread the energies of my own temper—tear him away, lest I stain my honour with the blood of her husband whom I adore.

ORLOFF.   I will not stir—Give way to all your vengeance—Vengeance would now be mercy.

IBRA.

IBRA. Amiſt the agonies I ſee thee in, thou art my envy! She is thy wife, ſhe ſurely loves thee, and pints to be reſtor'd to thy arms—By what tortures would I not purchaſe with ſuch a bliſs—Bear him off, I command—Yet hurt him not, but drag him from the harem.

ORLOFF. At your peril, ſlaves.

[*They drag him off.*]

IBRA. And now, oh wretched Ibrahim! what remains for thee? A moment ſince, the fruit of feliciry bent down within thy reach; the branches were loaden with happineſs, and thy joys bloom'd forth in tender bloſſoms; but a hurricane is come, the tree is torn up by the roots, and its fruits are devour'd by diſappointment.

TURK. Mighty Lord! is not the beauteous ſlave within thy power?

IBRA. Within my power! No, ſhe is removed from it for ever. As my ſlave, I have undoubted right over her; but as the wife of another, ſhe is ſacred.

MULEY. Then remove her from your preſence, and give her back to her adorning huſband.

IBRA. Never! O virtue, in exacting that, thy commands are too rigorous. Never, never can I ſend her from me—I will go this moment, and at her feet—Oh, I dare not—If I ſee her I am loſt—All barriers, human and divine, wou'd ſink before me—Beholding her within my graſp, and the dread of loſing her, would be a conflict in which *I* ſhou'd be loſt, and *ſhe* would be undone! I fly from her—I tear myſelf from the ſweet enchantment—Oh wretched huſband, I aſſume voluntarily the miſeries I have beſtow'd on thee!

[*Goes off wildly; on the ſide oppoſite that, at which* PAULINA *went.*]

TURK. What! run away from the woman he loves, when ſhe is in his power! She is *his*, and I would force her to make me happy.

MULEY. His generous ſpirit would abhor the deed! What, though his paſſions are headſtrong as the

mighty

mighty north; which shakes the pyramid to its base,
and lifts the rooted forest from the embracing earth,
yet will REFLECTION like a celestial minister arrive,
and scourge from his soul each spot and sordid tint,
that virtue ought to scorn, or manhood blush at.

[*Exeunt.*

·*Enter* FATIMA *and another Female Slave.*

FAT. Ah! this room is luckily empty. So, bring
in the Baffa's seat—We'll set it up here before it
goes to the pavilion; that we may judge of it—Come,
make haste.   [*speaking to those without*]

> [*Two or three bring in between them a light
> stool, on which is a white sattin covering,
> ornamented with festoons; another brings a
> small white sattin mattrass, trimm'd with
> gold fringe.*]

FAT. There, set the stool just there—Now put
on the covering—Give me the mattrafs—There, do
you see how nicely it fits? Now bring the canopy.

> [*Slaves bring in a canopy ornamented with fes-
> toons, gold fringe, and tassels.*]

Fix it just here—There—that will do—Is it not
pretty? [*walks round it*]

·2d. SLAVE. It is delightful! How charmed the
Baffa will be when he sees it in his pavilion at supper;
and he will praise both our industry and our taste.

FAT. Mercy! what's that noise?—Why—here
comes that impudent slave who was hanging over the
garden wall.

Enter several female Slaves hastily, followed by
A LA GREQUE.

A LA GR. My dear pretty little creatures, why do
you fly from me at this rate? Grant me one kiss to
save my life,—for I am famish'd.

·FAT. That kiss would *cost* thee thy life, should
it be known.

A LA GR. Known! [*getting to a small distance,
and speaking at rant*] Madam! what do you take
me for? Do you think that I, Madam, am a man to
betray

betray a lady's favours? I, who have been well receiv'd by duchesses and marchionesses?

FAT. [*interrupting him*] Duchesses and Marchionesses! What are they?

A LA GR. [*in his usual tone*] They were a sort of female creatures, my dear, who once infested Paris.

FAT. And where are they now?

A LA GR. Now, my sweet charmer, there is not one in the country, I mean of *native* growth; and if the neighbouring nations do not now and then send them one for a sample, a duchess will be as rare an animal in France, as a crocodile.—You sweet fellow! [*throwing his arm round* FATIMA]

FAT. You *bold* fellow! [*breaking from him*] Why you are quite at your ease.

A LA GR. I always am;—and I'll sit down on this pretty seat, and be quite comfortable.

FAT. You must not sit there—it is a seat made on purpose for the Bassa. [*Two or three endeavour to prevent him.*]

A LA GR. Well, can't you fancy *me* the Bassa? [*Sits.*]

Enter LAURETTA.

LAUR. Mercy! mercy! What, a man amongst ye? are ye all bewitched?

A LA GR. No; they have only bewitched me— Ah! you lively little rogue. [*flying to her*]—Come here, and sit down by me, and you shall be my Bassaess. I like you best of all.

LAUR. If you like your own life—Fly swifter than the light.

A LA GR. [*rising*] With *you* any where.

LAUR. Stranger, this is no place for gallantry, or for jesting; are you not afraid of death?

A LA GR. Afraid of him? No—Death is an aristocrate! and I am bound, as a Frenchman, to hate him.

AZIM.

AZIM. [*without*] Search every where, I say—He muſt be hereabout—I ſaw him aſcend.—Come this way.

LAUR. There! Now your careleſſneſs or your courage will be equally ineffectual. Unhappy ſtranger, you are on the threſhold of death.

[*The ſlaves clap their hands, and ſeem agoniz'd.*
1ſt. SLAVE. We too are loſt!

A LA GR. Not unleſs *I* am *found*. What a dozen women without a trick to ſave one man! Ah! I am ſenſible of my imprudence too late. [*Throws himſelf on his knees, turning firſt to one, then to another.*] Oh, ſave me! ſave me!

LAUR. What ſignifies your kneeling?—yet, it *ſhall* ſignify—Lower! [*puſhing him*] Lower ſtill! reſt on your hands—Reach that covering—quick—quick!

[*They cover him with the drapery, mattraſs, &c. and place the canopy behind him.*

AZIM. [*Without*] Come this way then—here he muſt have entered. [*Enters with others.*] Fly all of ye—hide yourſelves—A man is ſomewhere in the harem.

LAUR. And what are we to fly for? Is a man a tyger, that we ſhou'd be ſo ſcared? Who is he?

AZIM. The new French ſlave—Frenchmen, there is no being guarded againſt.—They make free every where.

LAUR. At leaſt they have made themſelves free AT HOME! and who knows, but, at laſt, the ſpirit they have raiſed may reach even to a Turkiſh harem, and the rights of women be declared, as well as thoſe of men.

AZIM. Don't talk to me of the rights of women —you would do *right* to go and conceal yourſelves as I order'd ye—You, Iſmael, and Hafez go and ſearch the inner apartments, I'll wait here, with the reſt, to intercept him, ſhould he eſcape ye.

[*Two ſlaves go off.*

LAUR. O, we'll intercept him, never fear—you'd better follow the reſt. [*Puſhing him*]

AZIM.

Azim. I choofe to wait here, and I'll fit down, for I'm horribly tired.

Laur. Pardon me, Mr. Azim—I am going to fit there myfelf, [*Sits, on A la Greque.*]

Azim. I fay I'll fit there, Madam, fo get up.

Laur. I wonder at your impertinence. Surely we may keep our feats, though we have loft our liberties.

Azim. I have been walking ever fince fun rife.

Laur. Then walk till it lets—Motion is healthful.

Azim. I fay I will fit down.—Give me the feat.

Laur. A fit-down I would give you with all my heart, and fuch a one as you fhould never forget ; but this feat you fhall not have.

Azim. Say you fo—I'll convince you in a moment. [*Goes to* Lauretta, *and feizes her hand to pull her up.*

Ism. [*Without*] We have found him—We have found him—There is a door faften'd on the infide—He muft be there.

Azim. Hah ! follow—follow—Now, we'll fhew a Frenchman what liberty is in Turkey.

[*Exit with the male flaves.* Lauretta *rifes*

A la Gr. [*Getting up with the covering about him.*] That fellow is certainly defcended from Cerberus, or an Englifh maftiff. My precious burden, how fhall I thank you ! Jupiter, when loaded with Europa on his back, was not half fo much charmed with her, as I am with you. [*Slaves fpeak without.*

Laur. Wafte not an inftant—They are returning— Begone

A la Gr. Well, good bye then, and heav'n blefs ye all, and fend to each LIBERTY and a HUSBAND ! [*They pufh him off.*

2d. *Slave.* What a kind man he is! How happy muft Frenchwomen be to have fuch lovers for hufbands.

Laur. Yes, my dear, they wou'd be fo ; but unluckily hufbands *forget* to be lovers—Let us run and
appeafe

appeafe Azim, you hear he is loud, and his vengeance
may fall upon us—Hafte—hafte!

[Exeunt haftily, all but FATIMA.

FAT. I'll make no hafte about it. [*Looking round
irrefolutely.*] Hang me if I don't try to change a
word or two with that agreeable Frenchman--I fhou'd
like to know a little of their cuftoms—Such an opportunity can't happen above once in one's life—So,
Monfieur Azim, ha, ha, ha! What a fool he is now.

[*Exit.*

SCENE, *The Garden.*

Enter IBRAHIM *from towards the Top, thoughtfully
follow'd at a fmall Diftance by* MULEY.—*He fighs
deeply.*

MULEY. Alas! my Lord, dare your flave offer
you confolation?

IBRA. I can receive none.

MULEY. I know that in afflictions like your's,
there can be but one fupport, that is in virtue—there,
my Lord——

IBRA. [*Interrupting*] Yes, I have refolv'd!—She
fhall be facred—her chaftity for ever inviolate! and
perhaps, [*fighing*] perhaps I may hereafter reftore her
to her hufband.

MULEY. That will be a moment of triumph to
yourfelf.--When magnanimity thus conquers affliction,
affliction may be envied.—Such a moment is the im-
primature of heaven on the purified heart—it is the
exaltation of virtue.

IBRA. O VIRTUE! when I can do that, thou
may'ft boaft a victory indeed! When I can refolve no
more to look on the foft radiance of her eyes—
When I can refolve to behold no more the natural and
unartful graces that adorn her—When I fhall feek
thofe groves in vain for that dear form; when I fhall
liften, and hear her voice no more—then, then, O
virtue! thou may'ft *boaft* thy triumph. [*After a
paufe.*]

pause] Leave me, for night and folitude beſt fuit the colour of my mind.   [*Exeunt.*

ORLOFF *appears at the top of the wall, where* A LA GREQUE *had before been ſeen, and calls to him.*]

ORLOFF. Quick, pri'thee! mount, and give me the rope—O! thou art as ſlow as if this moment were *not* the moſt precious of my life! As though this garden did *not* contain my Alexina.

A LA GR. [*Appearing*] Conſider, I have but juſt had one eſcape, my Lord, and another eſcape may eſcape *me*—There; here's the rope, if you will be ſo ventureſome—but don't blame me if they ſhould make you dangle at the end of it.

ORLOFF. [*takes the end of the rope, and is let down*] There! Environ'd with dangers as I am, this moment is dear to me, and the firſt, that for ſucceeding months has given my benighted foul one gleam of comfort.

A LA GR. Well, my Lord, I leave ye to your comfort—I am off—The very moon over my head ſeems to ſay, " Sweet Monſieur A la Greque, your maſter is very little better than a lunatic; ſo, take care of *yourſelf*"—I am off [*goes down*].

ORLOFF. Ye conſcious walks, which the feet of my Alexina have ſo often preſs'd, ye bending trees, whoſe boughs have given to her beauties your foft ſhade; ye fountains, whoſe murmurs have ſometimes lull'd her ſorrows to repoſe, my full foul greets ye! Hah! ſurely her voice floated on that paſſing breeze —No—all is ſtill. That paſſing breeze may bear upon it's wings a thouſand notes, but none like hers. O, thou pale moon, thou art not deck'd to-night in half thy glories; ſhine brighter, put on thy moſt ſeduçive rays, to tempt my angel from her ſad retirement! [*Soft muſic at a diſtance,*] Muſic in the gardens! Near that fpot then I ſhall not fail to find her —It is an abjuration her foul muſt yield to, for her foul is harmony. [*Exit. Muſic continues a few bars.*

PAU.

PAU. Where, where can the Baſſa conceal himſelf? I am tired with ſeeking him—Can he be offend-
ed with me, that he flies me thus? Alas! I feel I
could not *bear* to offend him—Oh, no, I *could* not!
[*Enter* MUSTAPHA.] Ah, Muſtapha, haſt thou ſeen
the Baſſa?

MUS. Not I—I have been taken up in watching
the motions of Azim, who, I am ſure, has ſome plot
in hand, though I cannot divine what—Where is the
gentle Alexina.

PAU. [*Pettiſhly*] I don't know—I hav'n't ſeen
her a great while.

MUS. Nor I—I'll go in queſt of her—Should the
Baſſa have ſeen her, I would not give a cockle-ſhell
for our ſcheme. [*Going.*] But what's the matter?
Why you look as diſmally as a widow at the funeral
of her thirteenth huſband.

PAU. I can't find the Baſſa—I have been looking
for him 'till my eyes ache—He flies me now, he does
indeed [*ſighing*].

MUS. Ay, ay, I underſtand it—You would put too
much honey on his bread, though I gave ye the
caution—You have been too kind to him.

PAU. [*with quickneſs*] I am ſure I have not.

MUS. Pho! pho! I know better—Have you not
learnt, child, that fondneſs is the moſt cloying food
in the world? Daſh your ſweet ſauce with acid, if
you would not have it pall upon the palate.

PAU. [*Angrily*] So I did then—I was as croſs
as I could poſſibly be—I never treated a gentleman ſo
hard harted before. To be ſure I muſt ſay, that at
leaving him, I told him—I told him he might *follow*
me. [*Confuſed*]

MUS. Ay, there's the caſe—You ivited him to
follow, and he in courſe runs away. [*Angrily*]

PAU. Oh dear! [*Takes out a fan to hide her
tears.*]

MUS. If I were a woman, wou'd *I* tell a man to
follow me? [*Snatches her fan.*] This is the away you
ſhou'd

fhou'd treat 'em—" Keep your diftance, Sir—how
" can you be fo rude? Fie! my Lord, it is quite
" fhocking! [*Very affected and extravagant with
" the motions of the fan.*] Oh, monftrous! if you
" come nearer I fhall faint! I hate you now, I do in-
" deed—I can't poffibly bear ye!" This, you fee,
would be graceful and captivating [*throwing away
the fan.*]

Pau. Graceful and captivating! [*With furprife*]

Mus. I tell ye, the women are all fools! and if
the fweet rogues knew what they loft by fubftituting
rouge for blufhing, and an undaunted look for modeft
timidity, we fhould foon fee all their affections fwal-
low'd by one, and that would be the affectation of
modefty.   [*Exit.*

Pau. I hate affectation—For all he thinks he
knows fo much, the next time I'll follow my own
way—I am fure I know as much of the matter as he
does.

Re-enter MUSTAPHA.

Mus. [*Peeping in through the wing.*] Remem-
ber the hint I gave you—if our mafter fhou'd fee
your countrywoman, all your hopes are gone in a
hurricane. You may as well attempt to catch a
hufband with bird-lime as to catch him after that; fo
prevent it.   [*Exit.*

Pau. How can I prevent it? Befides, Mr. Deftiny, I have good reafon to think, that as far as the
matter of beauty goes, I am not behind hand with fhe
—Alack-a-day! no, no, he has hit upon it!—As
fure as harveft is yellow, Lady Alexina has certainly
feen the Baffa, and he'll now be *her* ADORER as he
calls it—May be they are now together, and he is at
her feet fighing, as he did to-day at nine—Oh, I
cannot bear it—The fight wou'd crack my heart-
ftrings! Now I do feel that I dearly, dearly love
him—Oh mercy! he is here—he is here!

G   *Enter*

Enter IBRAHIM *musing; seeing* PAULINA, *starts.*

IBRA. Oh Paulina, l i'e thee, hide thee! At sight of thee every resolution fades, a d t e altar of virtue seems to blaze no more [*gazing on her long*]. Cruel charmer!

PAU. Cruel! Oh no, my heart melts to see your distress, and I am sure you have no occasion for it.

IBRA. Why didst thou not at first tell me thou wert another's! Why suffer my heart to burn with tumultuous love, to waste itself in glowing flames, whilst thine beats only for another.

PAU. What other?

PAU. *sings.*

" Never 'till now I felt love's dart——
" Guess who it was that stole my heart,
" 'Twas only you, if you'll believe me!" *

IBRA. O thou enchantress! [*Starting back.*] Thou wife of Orloff! thou hast my soul in chains—drag it not to perdition!

PAU. Why should you call me *wife of Orloff?* Oh, forgive me if I speak too plain—My heart, my whole heart is your's. You have awaken'd its first tender thought, and you shall fill it to the last! There *can* be no other.

IBRA. Nay then, farewel to every dread! Tho' hell shou'd gape beneath my feet, I *shrink* not—Rush on my soul, ALMIGHTY LOVE! absorb each faculty and thought, for I am thine!—[*turning to* PAU.]— *for* I am thine! [*Throws himself prone ; then rises and clasps her.*] Transcendent moment! O, bliss too exquisite!

ORLOFF. [*Rushes in*] Base woman! adulterous villain! [*Presents a dagger to* IBRAHIM's *breast.*]
PAULINA *shrieks and runs off.*

---

* These lines were introduced by Mrs. *Esten.*—She sings them without instruments, and they are always followed by rapturous applause.

IBRA.

IBRA. Hah! [*wrefts the dagger*] my life attack'd
—Ho! flaves! [*Slaves rufh in from various wings.*]
Twice to-day! Once in the bofom of my harem,
and now in the facred walks of my garden—Seize
him [*to the flaves, who obey*]. Thy death fhall
expiate thy double crime.

ORLOFF. Doft thou think to give me terror?—I
welcome death—I welcome it 'midft tortures!

IBRA. Chriftian, thou know'ft me not! Whilft
left to myfelf, I could command myfelf! My ardent
paffions I could hold in chains, and fupprefs that love
which honour could not fanction—But thou fhalt
know whe' thus oppos'd, I own no law but *will*—
drag him away. [*Exit.*

ORLOFF. Tyrant, I know that I fhall die; but
the bitternefs of death is paft—To live after having
feen my wife embrace thee, and embrac'd—Oh mad-
nefs! fpeed your death, I rufh to meet it.

[*Exeunt.*

SCENE, *The Prifon.*

Enter ALEXINA *through the Flat.*

ALEX. Surely this is the darkeft hour of the night!
The dim light my folitary window afforded has long
been paft, and gloom and filence every where prevail.
No found, no footftep, no voice of foft confoling love,
or weeping friendfhip. Can I be her whom the beamy
finger'd morn, till lately, ever rous'd to joy? I, her
who not a fhort hour fince glow'd with delight—
whofe troubled fky felicity and freedom began to gild?
Oh, the reverfe is too deep, too direful!

Voices [*without*] This way—make fure the outer
gate.

ALEX. Hah! flaves and lights! perhaps they
come to end my wretched being—Ah! nature fhrinks
at the idea, and whilft I almoft dread to live, I fly
from death, by impulfe irrefiftible!

[*Exit haftily through the flat.*

[ORLOFF *is brought in by flaves*]

SLAVE. There, Sir! Here you muft ftay till our mafter hath determined on the *fort* of death you are to die, for we have great variety in this country. The bowftring is the eafieft you can hope for. We'll leave you a lamp though, to fhew the apartments, and make your laft hours a little pleafant—Wifh your honour a good night.   [*Exeunt flaves.*

ORLOFF. May this hour of bitternefs be fhort! Here, on the flinty earth I'll pafs it, and give to thee —*defpair!* the fleeting moments that remain.
        [*Throws himfelf on the ground.*

ALEXINA *enters, fearful, from the flat.*

ALEX. What wretch can he be, who, in this dreary place, is the victim of tyranny and defpotifm? [*Advancing and looking over him.*] By every facred power it *is* my hufband! Orloff—[*feizing his hand*] my Orloff! [*He ftarts up, throws her off, and flies to the oppofite fide.*] Doft thou diftruft thy fenfes? It is thy Alexina—thy wretch'd—happy Alexina!

ORLOFF. Abandon'd woman! doft thou follow me to my prifon to infult my laft moments? Or doft thou come to adminifter the bowl of death?

ALEX. Heavens! what mean you? [*rufhing towards him with open arms.*]

ORLOFF. Nay, touch me not—By heav'n, rather than be enfolded in thy adulterous embrace, I'll— *draws a dagger*] O, my thoughts are defperate! Avoid me if thou would'ft live.

ALEX. Alas! affliction has made him mad.

ORLOFF. Oh! [*flings away the dagger.*]

ALEX Or if thou art not mad, to threaten death is needlefs. Be witnefs for me, ye celeftial fpirits, that I'll not live an inftant to endure a hufband's hate —All other miferies I've borne, but this laft fubdues me. [*fnatches up the dagger*] Thou accufeft me of
                                                    crimes

crimes I shudder at—Orloff, an adultress would not dare this blow.

ORLOFF. *springs forward, and seizes her arm*] Die! Yes, thou ought'st to die, but let my fate come first—It lingers not—its ministers are at hand! [*gazing on her*] O, had I not seen thee in his arms, had I not heard thy vows of never ending love to the tyrant.

ALEX. [*Interrupting eagerly.*] My vows! ah, my Orloff, a beam of radiance once more breaks in on my afflicted soul. I have never seen the Bassa—Nay, look not thus incredulous—this dungeon proves it—I am a prisoner here as well as you, and was this day brought hither.

ORLOFF. [*Gazing wildly*] Oh fate, spare me a moment! Scarcely dare I give way to the overpowering thought! yet it must be so! It was not thee, my heaven! whom I beheld in Ibrahim's arms—No, it was another, and Alexina's pure!

ALEX. As pure as at that sacred hour, when at the altar you receiv'd my virgin vows; and heaven is witness that this form has ne'er been press'd in any arms but thine.

ORLOFF. *Clasping her.*] Then art thou dearer in these prison walls, dearer in this thy faded beauty, than when a blaze of charms o'erpower'd my senses, beneath the haughty dome where first I woo'd thee.

ALEX. How matchless is the power of virtuous love! Having thus seen thee, having thus once again been press'd to thy fond bosom, I am prepar'd for death.

ORLOFF. Behold! they mean that we shou'd die together—The ministers of death are entering.

[*Going towards the wing.*]

MUS. [*Without.*] Make fast the outer gate—bring him along. [*Entering Slaves bring in* AZIM, *in chains; they are followed by* LAURETTA, FATIMA, *and females; male slaves bearing torches.*] I thought we should nick you at last. The lime twigs which you have been so busily spreading for another, have at length entangled thyself.

LAUR.

LAUR. Yes, my friend Azim ; I promis'd you a *fet down*, and now I think you will have it. Joy—joy to Alexina !

MUS. To Alexina and her lord.

ORLOFF. Ah ! what mean ye ? A tide of bliſs breaks in upon my ſoul, which *yet* I dare not yield to.

LAUR. Fear not to truſt it ! Our maſter hath heard from Paulina your touching ſtory, and hath ſent us to conduct you to his preſence.

MUS. Go, Madam! and make room for your perſecutor AZIM ;—*be* ſhall take your place here.

ALEX. Farewel—farewel, ye dreary walls ! We fly to light, to liberty——

ORLOFF. To love !

[*Exit, leading* ALEXINA, *followed by part of the ſlaves.*

MUS. [*To Azim.*] Why you look a little ſtrange ; —pray make free, Sir ; you are as welcome as though you were at home. [*Bowing ludicrouſly.*]

LAUR. Come, hold up your head, man ! and look round your now apartments. Examine the furniture —is it not elegant ! Look through its ſpacious windows—are you not charm'd with the proſpect ? Thou monſter ! to this dreary abode thou wouldſt have conſign'd innocence and virtue.

AZIM. O, that thoſe curſed chains were off !—*I* to be impriſon'd in a dungeon !

MUS. Come, come—" a few weeks ſpent here " will quiet you a little." I have heard every thing from your accomplice there. " Your ſorrows won't " be half ſo violent a fortnight hence, as they are " now—let that comfort ye."

AZIM. [*Furiouſly.*] Dogs !

MUS. Be civil, and " I'll permit thee to uſe the " apartment next to this—its laſt inhabitant had it " fourteen years," you know. [*Tauntingly.*] Nay, it is in vain to ſtruggle, drag him in ! [*Exit.*

[*Slaves*

[*Slaves drag* AZIM *in* ; *the door is shut.*]

LAUR. Ah! he's caught at laft. [*Runs up to the door.*] Good night, my pretty Azim. [*He rattles his chains.*] Good night—I'll give ye a friendly call once a month or fo, for the next ten years. [*He rattles.*] Farewel—pleafant fancies hang about your dreams! [*Exit; followed by the flaves with torches* ; AZIM *rattling his chains within.*]

SCENE, *The Baffa's Apartment.*

Enter IBRAHIM *at top, leading* PAULINA.

IBRA. O, adored Paulina! what wonderful events are thefe! Thou *may'ft* be mine! it is no *crime* to love thee. I have ftruggled againft a paffion which heaven had determin'd to reward.

PAU. It bleffes my heart to fee you fo happy! And fhall my father and brother be releas'd from flavery—fhall they *witnefs* my happinefs?

IBRA. They fhall *partake* it. Riches and honour await thofe fo dear to thee. Lo! they are here.

[*The father and fon are introduced.*

PAU. O, my dear father! Peter! what a day this has been! Here am I going to be a great lady, and not the handmaid of a Jew, as you told me this morning. [*To her father.*]

FATHER. My dear child, I cannot fpeak for joy. Say fomething for us to the Baffa—we fhrink before him.

ALEX. [*Without.*] Haften!—O, my Orloff, let us haften to his prefence. [*Entering.*] Mighty Ibrahim, I no longer tremble to appear before thee;—in the prefence of my hufband, I dare to *look* upon thee, and to afk thy mercy.

IBRA. Mercy! how poor the word! I give ye inftant liberty, and in giving ye that, I give ALL, for ye *love*! What then remains to perfect your blifs!

ORLOFF.

ORLOFF. Hearest thou, ALEXINA? Ah! what sounds—they rush upon my soul in transport.

IBRA. Valiant Russian, I embrace thee! The poniard you directed to my breast, had it enter'd there, would have pierc'd a heart, which, amidst the turbulencies of war, and the infatuations of a court, has yet preserv'd its OWN RESPECT;—accept its friendship!

ORLOFF. With earnestness unspeakable; and I return it with such gratitude and fervour, as becomes a soldier and a husband.

IBRA. Such charms, I could not have beheld infensibly. [to Alexina] had I known them before Paulina engrossed my heart—but now, that heart can beat for her alone. To-morrow you shall be escorted to your camp, and I, to give that dignity to love, without which it sinks into lowest appetite, will make this charmer mine, by sacred rites.

ORLOFF. Illustrious Turk! Love has taught thee to revere marriage, and marriage shall teach thee to honour love.

A LA GR. Why what ups and downs there are in this world! My lord, [to Orloff, I am once again your most duteous servant—for fellow slaves, I perceive we shall be no longer —So there goes my dignity! I'll make a bold push for a new one though. Azim, I find——pardon me, my lord, [to Ibrahim] Azim, I find, is out of place, will your mightiness bestow it on me, and make me your principal slave-driver?

IBRA. [Laughing.] What wouldst thou do?

A LA GR. Any thing, and every thing. I'd imitate the smack of Azim's whip, and roll my eyes as he does, to frighten your male slaves, and transform myself into a sattin seat, with a canopy over my head, to amuse your female slaves.

IBRA. Transform thyself into a sattin seat, with a canopy over thy head—thou art bewildered. [To Alexina.] Pronounce, Madam, the fate of the profligate slave, whose villainy had nearly brought about such disastrous events—Shall he perish?

ALEX.

ALEX. Ah, in this hour of felicity, let nothing perish but *misfortune!* Be the benevolent Muftapha rewarded, and let Azim have frank forgivenefs.

IBRA. Charming magnanimity! if it flows from your CHRISTIAN DOCTRINES, fuch doctrines muft be RIGHT, and I will clofely ftudy them.

ALEX. [*Stepping forward.*] And may our errors have frank forgivenefs too! Beftow on us your favour, and make the DAY IN TURKEY one of the happieft of this happy feafon!

THE END.

EPILOGUE.

WRITTEN BY MRS. COWLEY.

SPOKEN BY MRS. POPE.

ESCAP'D from Turkey, and from prison free,
Yet still a SLAVE you shall behold in me;
An *English* slave—slave to your ev'ry pleasure,
Seeking your plaudits as her richest treasure.

Whilst thus you feast with cheering praise my ear,
For our soft poet I confess some fear.
Perhaps you'll say,—" Two marriages for love !
" Thus foolish *female* pens for ever rove ;
" But give us, Madam, give us, *real* life,
" Who goes to Turkey pray, to fetch a wife?"

Critic ! a few months past I wou'd allow
Your comment just, but not, Sir Surly, now !
For now we know A PRINCE can cross the seas
T' obtain a wife, a nation's hearts to please.
" *The age of chivalry*" again returns,
And love, with all its ancient splendour burns ;
Yes——
Tell the rapt Orator whose magic pen
So late chastised the new found rights of men——
Who fear'd that honour, courage, love were lost,
And Europe's glories in the whirlwind tost ;
Tell him " *heroic enterprise*" shall still survive,
And " *loyalty to sex*" remain alive ;
" *The unbought grace of life*" again we find,
And " *proud submission*" fills the public mind ;
T'wards *her*, now borne to BRITAIN's happy coast—
A husband's honour, and a nation's boast.

" *Just*

" *Juſt lighted on this orb the viſion ſhines*
" *Scarce ſeems to touch*," and as it moves, refines !
O, may ſhe long adorn this choſen iſle,
Where the beſt gifts of fate unceaſing ſmile !
When, " *like the morning ſtar*" at wond'rous height,
She ſoars at length beyond this world and night,
Still may your bleſſings to her name be given,
While ſoft ſhe fades into her native heaven !

THOSE who *read* will know, that in the above Epilogue
all the paſſages diſtinguiſhed by italics are taken from an
effuſion inſpired by *another* royal lady; — agitating the
lightning pen of a man who in his head is all REASON, in
his heart all SENSATION. A man whom *politics* ſeized, and
ſeems to have dragged reluctantly from LOVE. Let the
women of future times weave to his memory the faireſt gar-
lands, and twine amidſt laurels and roſes the name of BURKE.

THE canopy is compofed of two umbrellas of white fattin, or ftuff; the upper one very fmall, each trimmed with gold fringe, feftoons of flowers, and taffels. The covering for the ftool, of the fame materials, is made in the form of a hammer cloth; a white fatin mattrefs is laid on it, trimmed with gold fringe.

www.ingramcontent.com/pod-product-compliance
Lightning Source LLC
Chambersburg PA
CBHW020329090426
42735CB00009B/1458